Power*base*

Elementary

Longman

David Evans

1 introductions

HELLO

1 Introduce yourselves.

> Hello. I'm …
>
> Hello. I'm …

2 How many English words or phrases do you know that mean *hello*? Write them down and practise saying them to each other.

hello

INTRODUCING YOURSELF

3 Listen and match what the people say to the pictures on these pages. Then check with your partner.

> Good morning. It's 10 o'clock and this is the news. I'm Patricia da Gama.

> Hello. This is Ravi Shipman. I'm not here at the moment, but please leave your name and number. Thank you.

> Good evening. This is your captain speaking. My name's Roger Harper. Welcome aboard …

> Hello. I'm David. Pleased to meet you.

> Good afternoon. It's Paul de Gromoboy here. I'm from International Media.

4 Look at the speech bubbles again and <u>underline</u> the four different ways of telling someone your name.

CONTEXTS 5 Match these situations to the pictures.

on the phone   in a meeting   on TV
on an answerphone   a pilot on a plane

NOW YOU 6 Introduce yourself to other people in the class, using one of the phrases on these pages. The other person guesses the context. Do this with as many people as possible.

Good afternoon. It's Julia here.   *You're on the phone.*

G R A M M A R *to be*

WHO ARE THEY? **1** Read what these people say. Then answer the questions.

Hi. I'm Patrizio Bertelli.

Hello. I'm Miuccia Prada.

We're from Italy. We're in the fashion business.

1 Who is she?
   She's Miuccia Prada.

2 Who is he?
   _____

3 Where are they from?
   _____

4 What business are they in?
   _____

A HOLLYWOOD COUPLE **2** Use the information below to write sentences about these people. Use *he, she* and *they.*

Name	Jennifer Aniston
Country	USA
Business	Movie business

Name	Brad Pitt
Country	USA
Business	Movie business

She's Jennifer Aniston ...

CHECK *to be*

➕	➖	❓	Short answers
I'm	I'm not	Am I ... ?	Yes, I am. / No, I'm not.
You're	You aren't	Are you ... ?	Yes, you are. / No, you're not.
He/She/It's	He isn't	Is he ... ?	Yes, he is. / No, he isn't.
We/You/They're	We aren't	Are we ... ?	Yes, we are. / No, we aren't.

NEGATIVES AND QUESTIONS

3 Make true sentences. Fill the gaps with the positive or negative form of *to be*.

1 Patrizio Bertelli _isn't_ from Germany.
2 I _____ from Japan.
3 Jennifer Aniston _____ from the USA.
4 I _____ in the movie business.
5 Miuccia and Patrizio _____ in the fashion business.
6 Brad and Jennifer _____ in the travel business.

4 👥 Make questions from the sentences above. Reply with short answers.

> Is Patrizio Bertelli from Germany?   No, he isn't.

ASKING QUESTIONS

5 👥 Put these words in the correct order to make questions. Compare your questions with your partner.

1 from / Brad Pitt / is / where ?   *Where is Brad Pitt from?*
2 business / what / Miuccia Prada / in / is ?   _____
3 you / from / Russia / are ?   _____
4 from / they / where / are ?   _____
5 Jennifer and Brad / business / in / what / are ?   _____
6 he / in / is / the movie business ?   _____

NOW YOU

6 Write your country and your business on the note. (Use a dictionary to help you.)

> I'm from ...
>
> I'm in ...

7 👥 Ask and answer questions about your country and your business.

> Where are you from?   What business are you in?

8 👥 Talk about other people in the class. Ask about their countries and their businesses.

working life *Contacts*

A FIRST MEETING

1 🎧 Read and listen to this conversation. Then <u>underline</u> three pairs of phrases which have similar meanings.

■ Pedro, I'd like you to meet Tanya.

○ How do you do?

■ Tanya, this is Pedro.

▲ Pleased to meet you.

○ So, Tanya, which company are you with?

▲ I'm with Telecom International. Who do you work for?

○ The same company. Telecom International!

2 👥👥👥 Work in groups of three and read the conversation. Use your names and the names of your companies.

MEETING A FRIEND

3 🎧 Listen and fill the gaps with these words.

to see	how's	Fine	thank you	How are	see you

■ Teresa! Good *to see* _____ you again. How are you?

○ _____ , thank you. _____ you?

■ Very well, _____ . So, _____ business?

○ Oh, OK. I'm very busy at the moment.

■ Good to hear it. Anyway, _____ soon!

○ Yes, see you!

4 👥👥 Have a similar conversation to the one above. Ask and answer these questions.

How are you?   *How's business?*

ON THE PHONE **5** Put this conversation in the right order. Then listen and check.

Just a moment, please. … I'm sorry, she's not in the office today. ☐

It's Raymond Merope, from Atlas Products. ☐

Of course. What's your name, please? ☐

Hello, Telecom International. *1*

Oh, hello. Can I speak to Dorota Celaeno, please? ☐

Oh, OK. No problem. Goodbye. ☐

6 Read the conversation above. Use your names and the names of your companies.

E-MAIL **7** Read this e-mail. Put in three full stops, nine capital letters and one question mark.

> hi claudio,
>
> my name's maia i'm new in the company my phone number's 555 8786
>
> how about a meeting some time soon
>
> regards,
>
> maia

8 Underline the words or phrases in the e-mail that you can replace with these phrases.

Best wishes   **Dear**   **Can we have**

9 Write e-mails to each other. Say where you're from and the business that you're in, and give your phone number. Then ask for a meeting next week.

real world *Numbers*

THE NEWS **1** 🎧 👥 Listen to the news and number the people or things in the order that you hear them.

◻ The dollar and the euro

◻ Football: Manchester United v Galataseray

1 Problems for George W Bush

◻ The stock market

◻ Hollywood film star Angelina Jolie

◻ Roskilde rock festival

NUMBERS IN THE NEWS

2 🎧 Listen to the news again and tick (✓) the correct answer to these questions.

1 What's the time?

| 4:00 | 8:00 | 10:00 | 12:00 |

2 How many days is George W Bush in Japan for?

1   3   5   7

3 How many people are at Roskilde in Denmark?

1,000   10,000   100,000   200,000

4 How many seconds are there in the name of Angelina Jolie's film?

2   16   20   60

5 How many points is the stock market up?

39   47   84   155

6 How many cents is the euro down?

78   8   14   80

7 What's the football result?

1 – 0   2 – 2   4 – 2   5 – 3

3 👥 Take turns to ask and answer the questions above.

4 👥 Match the following to the numbers and times above.

seven	_7_	ten thousand	_____
seventy-eight	_____	a hundred and fifty-five	_____
five – three	_____	twelve o'clock	_____
four o'clock	_____	sixteen	_____

NOW YOU

5 👥 **A** Say five numbers to B (they can be numbers on this page or others).
B Write them down. Read your numbers to check.

Swap roles.

PRONUNCIATION
/ɪ/ /iː/ /e/ /eɪ/

A 🎧 Listen and repeat. Notice the underlined vowel sounds.

/ɪ/	/iː/	/e/	/eɪ/
s<u>i</u>x	thr<u>ee</u>	t<u>e</u>n	<u>ei</u>ght
f<u>i</u>fty	thirt<u>ee</u>n	tw<u>e</u>nty	<u>ei</u>ghteen

B 🎧 Listen and repeat these words. Which phonemic symbol goes with the underlined sounds?

m<u>ee</u>ting	s<u>ee</u>	pl<u>ea</u>se	_____
n<u>a</u>me	pl<u>a</u>ne	tod<u>ay</u>	_____
f<u>i</u>lm	b<u>u</u>siness	capt<u>ai</u>n	_____
w<u>e</u>ll	f<u>e</u>stival	h<u>e</u>llo	_____

2 people

PEOPLE AND PLACES

1 👥 Write these words in the correct group.

> boss   hotel   manager   home   shop
> businessman   office   businesswoman
> factory   employee   customer   city

people

places

PLURALS

2 👥 Write the plural forms of these words.

home	_____	factory	_____
hotel	_____	boss	_____
employee	_____	city	_____

> **CHECK** Regular plurals
>
> For most words, add -*s*.   hotel → hotel**s**
> If the word ends in -*s*, add -*es*.   boss → boss**es**
> If the word ends in -*y*, add -*ies*.   city → cit**ies**

3 👥 Complete this table of irregular plurals.

SINGULAR	person		
PLURAL		men	women

PRONUNCIATION
/s/ /z/

🎧 Listen. Is the <u>underlined</u> sound in these words an /s/ sound or a /z/ sound? Write *s* or *z* next to each word.

bo<u>ss</u> *s*   bu<u>s</u>iness *z*   <u>c</u>ity   cu<u>s</u>tomer   employee<u>s</u>   factorie<u>s</u>
offi<u>c</u>e   manager<u>s</u>   per<u>s</u>on   shop<u>s</u>

A JAPANESE BUSINESSWOMAN

4 🎧 Listen and fill the gaps in this text.

Hanae Mori is from Japan and her
_____homes_____ are in Paris and Tokyo.
She's in the fashion business and she's the
_____ of Hanae Mori International.
It's an international company with
hundreds of _____ . Her clothes are
for _____ and her _____ are
from many different countries. She has
_____ in many of the world's big
_____ , including New York, Paris
and Tokyo.

NOW YOU

5 👥 Use the information below and the words on these pages to write sentences about this businessman. (Use *he* and *his* instead of *she* and *her*.) Then compare your sentences with your partner.

Name	Stelios Haji-Ioannou
Country	Greece
Business	Airline
Job	Chairman
Company	easyJet

Number of employees
1,500
Offices
London, Athens,
New York ...

His name's Stelios Haji-Ioannou.
_____
_____
_____
_____

_____

GRAMMAR Possessive adjectives

BUSINESS FAMILIES

1 Complete the table with these words.

son   sister   husband   mother

MAN	father		brother	
WOMAN		wife		daughter

2 Look at the pictures below. Point to the people and talk about the relationships between them.

I think she's his sister.

I think he's her brother.

3 Read the texts and find out if you're right.

Rupert

The *New York Post*, *The Times* of London and Sky TV are all part of News Corp. It's a huge media company, but it's also a family business. Its boss is an Australian, Rupert Murdoch; his number three is his son, Lachlan. Lachlan's brother, James, is also a top manager in the company, and their sister, Elizabeth, is a manager in the media business, too.

Lachlan, Elizabeth and James

Sofia and Spike

Francis

Sofia Coppola is from Hollywood's number one family. Her father is Francis Ford Coppola. He's the director of many famous movies, including *Apocalypse Now* and *The Godfather*. Nicolas Cage, who's a big film star, is also part of their family.

Sofia's husband is Spike Jonze, the director of the movie *Being John Malkovich*, and, of course, Sofia is a successful film director, too!

WHO'S WHO? **4** 👥 Take turns to ask and answer these questions.

1 Who's Lachlan Murdoch's sister?   *Elizabeth Murdoch*
2 Who's his brother?   _____
3 Who's Sofia Coppola's husband?   _____
4 Who's her father?   _____

5 👥 Look at the questions again. Which *'s* means *is* and which *'s* is possessive?

6 👥 Find examples of *'s* for *is* and *'s* for possessive in the texts opposite.

> **CHECK** Apostrophe *s*
>
> Who's he? = Who is he?   He's John. = He is John.
> Elizabeth's brother = the brother of Elizabeth

7 Rewrite these questions using *his, her, its* or *their*.

1 Who's Spike Jonze's wife?   *Who's his wife?*
2 Who's Elizabeth Murdoch's father?   _____
3 Who's Francis Ford Coppola's daughter?   _____
4 Who's News Corp's boss?   _____
5 Who's Lachlan and James's sister?   _____

> **CHECK** Possessive adjectives
>
> | I | **my** | he | **his** | we | **our** |
> |---|---|---|---|---|---|
> | you | **your** | she | **her** | you | **your** |
> | | | it | **its** | they | **their** |

NOW YOU **8** 👥 Take turns to ask and answer questions about Rupert Murdoch.

What / job?   Who / sons?
Where / from?   Who / daughter?

What's his job?

9 👥 Take turns to ask and answer more questions about the people in the texts opposite. Then ask about each other's families.

working life *Personal information*

A BUSINESS CARD **1** Look at this woman's business card. Draw a line from the question to the information that it asks for.

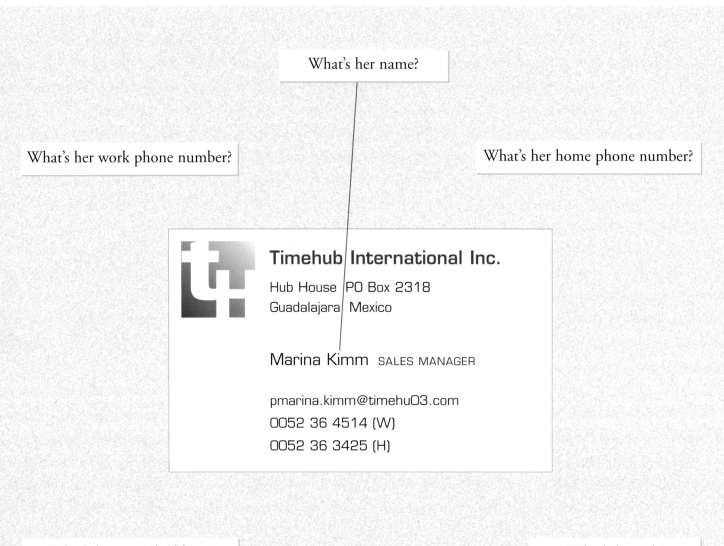

What's her name?

What's her work phone number?

What's her home phone number?

Timehub International Inc.

Hub House PO Box 2318
Guadalajara Mexico

Marina Kimm SALES MANAGER

pmarina.kimm@timehu03.com
0052 36 4514 (W)
0052 36 3425 (H)

What's her e-mail address?

What's her job?

What's her company's address?

Which company is she from?

2 Take turns to ask and answer the questions.

CAN YOU SPELL THAT?

3 🎧 Listen and repeat the letters of the alphabet.

Aa Bb Cc Dd Ee Ff Gg Hh Ii
Jj Kk Ll Mm Nn Oo Pp Qq Rr
Ss Tt Uu Vv Ww Xx Yy Zz

CHECK E-mail

@ = at
• = dot

4 👥 Look at the business card opposite and take turns to ask and answer these questions.

Can you spell her name?

Can you spell her company's name?

Can you spell her company's address?

Can you spell her e-mail address?

ASKING QUESTIONS

5 👥 Take turns to ask and answer questions.

A Look at the woman's business card on page 94.
B Ask the questions on the opposite page and write down A's answers. Ask these questions if you need to.

Can you spell that, please?

Can you speak more slowly, please?

Can you say that again, please?

B Look at the man's business card on page 97.
A Ask the questions on the opposite page and write down B's answers. (Remember this is a man's card, so use *his* instead of *her*.)

NOW YOU

6 👥 Make a business card for your partner. Ask questions to get the information you need. Then write and design the card.

PRONUNCIATION
/ɒ/ /əʊ/ /ʌ/

A 🎧 Listen and repeat. Notice the underlined vowel sounds.

/ɒ/	/əʊ/	/ʌ/
j<u>o</u>b	ph<u>o</u>ne	n<u>u</u>mber
d<u>o</u>t	sl<u>o</u>wly	c<u>o</u>mpany

B 🎧 Listen to these pairs of words. Do the underlined letters sound the same (✓) or different (✗)?

h<u>o</u>tel   – h<u>o</u>me   cl<u>o</u>thes   – fr<u>o</u>m
c<u>u</u>stomer – c<u>ou</u>ntry   wh<u>a</u>t   – sh<u>o</u>p
b<u>o</u>ss   – s<u>o</u>n   h<u>u</u>sband – m<u>o</u>ther
T<u>o</u>kyo   – L<u>o</u>ndon   br<u>o</u>ther   – cl<u>o</u>ck

real world

Food and drink

BUSINESS LUNCH **1** Talk about where you have lunch. Use these words.

at home   in a restaurant   in a café   in the company canteen
in a sandwich bar   at my desk

Where do you have lunch?   *I have lunch …*

2 Look at the picture. Which food and drink words do you know in English? Make a list.

A SANDWICH BAR **3** 🎧 Listen to a conversation in a sandwich bar. What does the person order to eat and drink?

4 🎧 👥 Listen again and then fill the gaps with the phrases in the boxes.

ASSISTANT ■

Can you say that again, please? **How about**
Thank you very much. **Can I help you?**

CUSTOMER ○

I'd like **Can I have**
what's this? **How much is it?**

■ Yes. _____

○ Hello. _____ a chicken sandwich, please.

■ Just chicken?

○ Er ... well, _____

■ That's avocado. It's very good with chicken.

○ Hmm. Avocado. And what are those?

■ Those are prawns.

○ OK. _____ a chicken and prawn sandwich?

■ _____ some tomatoes with that?

○ Tomatoes? Hmm. OK. Why not?

■ Right. One chicken, prawn and tomato sandwich!

○ And I'd like an orange as well, please.

■ Sorry. _____

○ I'd like an orange juice as well.

■ One orange juice!

○ _____

■ It's $5.50. _____

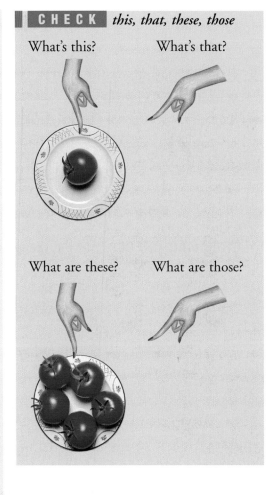

C H E C K *this, that, these, those*

What's this?   What's that?

What are these?   What are those?

NOW YOU **5** 👥 Role play this situation, using some of the language on these pages.

A You are a customer. Look at the picture opposite. Order a sandwich and a drink. If you don't know the English word, point and ask *What's this?*

B You are an assistant. Turn to page 100 for information.

Swap roles. (**A** Turn to page 100. **B** You are a customer.)

review 1

**VOCABULARY
Wordsearch**

1 Go down ↓ and across → to find at least 14 words from Units 1 and 2 in this square.

E	M	P	L	O	Y	E	E
F	U	H	L	U	N	C	H
A	Z	O	A	S	H	O	P
S	A	N	D	W	I	C	H
H	M	E	D	I	A	S	O
I	P	E	R	C	F	O	T
O	G	N	E	I	M	R	E
N	S	I	S	T	E	R	L
B	O	S	S	Y	N	Y	E

GRAMMAR CHECK

2 Fill the gaps with the correct forms of *to be*.

1 Excuse me. _Are you_____ Paula?
   No, _____ . I'm Claudia.
2 What business _____ they in?
   _____ in the fashion business.
3 What _____ your e-mail address?
   _____ seyu09@gho.net .
4 _____ from Japan?
   No, _____ . She's from Sweden.
5 Where _____ we?
   I'm not sure, but I think _____ in Kansas.

3 Fill the gaps with the correct possessive adjectives.

1 What's _your___ phone number?   _____ number's 6568 098.
2 What's _____ job?   He's a manager.
3 What's _____ name?   She's Elizabeth.
4 Where's _____ hotel?   We're at the Holiday Inn.
5 What's _____ address?   They're at 178 Main Street.

FOCUS ON ...
Articles

4 Which words go with *a* and which words go with *an*?

_a_ factory	_an_ office	_a_ company
____ employee	____ manager	____ customer
____ name	____ address	____ number
____ tomato	____ avocado	____ egg

5 When do we use *a/an* and *the*? Look at these sentences.

Rupert Murdoch is **a** businessman.
Rupert Murdoch is **the** boss of News Corp.

We say *a businessman* because there are a lot of other businessmen in the world. We say ***the boss*** because there is only one boss of News Corp.

■ Can I have **a** cup of coffee, please?
○ Of course. Here you are.
■ How much is **the** coffee?

We use *a/an* when you say something for the first time. We use *the* when we say it again.

6 Circle the correct articles in *italics* in these sentences.

1 Can I have ⓐ / *the* cheese sandwich, please?
2 What do you do? I'm *a* / *the* businesswoman.
3 What's *a* / *the* name of your boss?
4 It's *an* / *the* international company.
5 I'm sorry, she's not in *an* / *the* office today.

PRONUNCIATION
/b/ and /p/   /h/ and /j/

A 🎧 Listen and repeat. Notice the <u>underlined</u> sounds.

/b/		/p/	
<u>b</u>usiness	<u>b</u>est	<u>p</u>erson	<u>p</u>lace

B 🎧 Listen and repeat these phrases. Concentrate on the /b/ and /p/ sounds.

A plate of prawns, please.   My boss's brother's bar.
Help, please! It's a big problem.

C 🎧 Listen and repeat. Notice the <u>underlined</u> sounds.

/h/		/j/	
<u>h</u>er	<u>wh</u>o	<u>y</u>our	<u>U</u>SA

D 🎧 Listen and repeat these phrases. Concentrate on the /h/ and /j/ sounds.

Who's your new employee?   Do you have a home in the USA?
Yes, we have your number here.

3 jobs

JOB ADVERTS

1 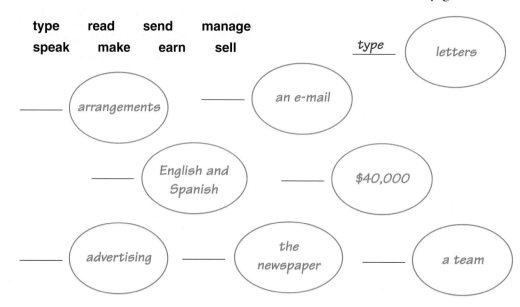 Look quickly at the adverts opposite and fill the gaps with these jobs.

> **accountant**   **secretary**   **salesperson**
> **manager**   **teacher**   **shop assistant**

BUSINESS VERBS

2 Look at the adverts again and find two more verbs which mean *phone*.

_____   _____

3 Find these verbs in the adverts. Which words in the circles do they go with?

> **type**   **read**   **send**   **manage**
> **speak**   **make**   **earn**   **sell**

type _____ (letters)

_____ (arrangements)   _____ (an e-mail)

_____ (English and Spanish)   _____ ($40,000)

_____ (advertising)   _____ (the newspaper)   _____ (a team)

4 Look again at the verbs in the box. Which other words in the circles can they go with?

TWO CALLS

5 Listen to part of two phone conversations. Which of the jobs opposite are the people calling about?

NOW YOU

6 Write sentences about your job, using the verbs on these pages. Then compare with a partner.

I send e-mails. _____   _____   _____

JOBS

Big book shop
in central Manchester

•

Three days a week

•

Good salary and benefits
Call Nick on
0161 8977 7866

In some jobs, you just type letters, make arrangements and read the newspaper – but not in this job!

In this job, you help with every part of office life. Every day is different, but the work never stops!

Interested?

Phone 0978 987601.

€20,000

An opportunity for the right

OK. You understand Excel and you're good with money. But are you the right person for us?

The right person is helpful and friendly. He or she knows the oil industry and speaks English and Spanish.

He or she also earns $65,000 a year! Is that person you?

Ring Carole on 00 3245 2345 or send an e-mail to carolep@eeb.com.

A fantastic future in Berlin

Office

€34,000 pa

Good communication skills? Good English, French and German? Three years in business on the Internet? Yes?

Then join us and manage a team of twelve people in our Berlin offices. We are a top Internet company with a fantastic future. Send an e-mail now to gretahj@intgo.co.de or call 987987 888.

Telephone

My name's Trevor Gibbons. I'm 22 years old and I earn $40,000 a year. How?

I sell advertising for an international newspaper.

Find out more.
Call me on 0207 555 6545.

WANTED

A piano
for the Carbone International School for Girls

☎ 8978 898921

GRAMMAR Present simple

A MANAGER'S WORKING LIFE

1  Read this newspaper article about Ian Eldridge, boss of PizzaExpress. Tick (✓) the sentences below which are true.

I don't have an office. My briefcase is my office. And I don't have a secretary. I do everything myself. I prefer it that way. I book my flights, I make my travel arrangements, I make my calls and I write my letters.

The Independent Business Review *4.4.01*

1 He has a big office.
2 He doesn't have a secretary.
3 He books his flights.
4 His secretary makes his travel arrangements.
5 He doesn't write letters.

YOUR WORKING LIFE

2 Write true sentences about yourself. Use these words.

1 have an office   _____
2 have a secretary   _____
3 make my travel arrangements   _____
4 make my calls   _____
5 write my letters   _____

CHECK Present simple			
⊕	⊖	❓	**Short answers**
I work	I don't work	Do I work?	Yes, I do. / No, I don't.
You work	You don't work	Do you work?	Yes, you do. / No, you don't.
He works	He doesn't work	Does he work?	Yes, he does. / No, he doesn't.
We work	We don't work	Do we work?	Yes, we do. / No, we don't.

❘ *Grammar reference page 105* ❘

PIZZAEXPRESS   **3** 👥 Read this article about PizzaExpress and circle the correct form of the verbs in *italics*.

PIZZAEXPRESS

As the boss of PizzaExpress, Ian Eldridge *don't have / doesn't have* a lot of free time. Around 7,000 people *work / works* for his company and it *have / has* more than 300 restaurants around the world – from Washington DC, to Paris, to New Delhi, to Tokyo.

Ian Eldridge *think / thinks* that PizzaExpress is a special company. Jazz musicians often *play / plays* in its restaurants and its employees are always friendly. But, of course, pizza is the really important thing at PizzaExpress.

'You just *don't find / doesn't find* our kind of pizza in other restaurants,' he *say / says*.

4 👥 Fill the gaps in these questions and write short answers.

1 __Does__ Ian Eldridge have a lot of free time?
  No, he doesn't. _____

2 _____ around 7,000 people work for his company?
  _____

3 _____ the company have more than 300 restaurants?
  _____

4 _____ rock musicians often play at its restaurants?
  _____

5 _____ Ian Eldridge think the company is special?
  _____

NOW YOU   **5** 👥 Take turns to ask and answer questions about your working life.

> *Do you have an office?*

> *Do a lot of people work for your company?*

> *Does your company have offices around the world?*

working **life** *Arrangements*

A MANAGER'S DIARY

1 Find these times in the sentences below and write them in numbers.

seven forty-five   *7:45*   eleven fifteen   _____

quarter to nine   _____   quarter past ten   _____

three thirty   _____   half past one   _____

1 Philippe always has a breakfast meeting with his secretary at 8:45 on Monday morning.

2 He never arrives in the office before 11:15 on Tuesday.

3 He always has lunch with a customer at 1:30 on Wednesday.

4 He sometimes has dinner with his team at 7:45 on Thursday evening.

5 He always has a meeting with his boss at 3:30 on Friday afternoon.

6 He sometimes plays golf at 10:15 on Saturday morning.

7 He never works on Sunday.

2 Read the sentences above about Philippe Sebald's working routine and make notes in his diary. If an arrangement is not definite, put a question mark (?) next to it.

CHECK Adverbs of frequency		
never	sometimes	always
0%		100%

21 Monday *8:45 Breakfast meeting with secretary*	**24** Thursday
22 Tuesday	**25** Friday
23 Wednesday	**26** Saturday
	27 Sunday

PRONUNCIATION
/m/ /n/

Listen and repeat these phrases. Concentrate on the /m/ and /n/ sounds.

a <u>m</u>eeting on <u>M</u>onday <u>m</u>orning   <u>n</u>ever <u>in</u> the after<u>n</u>oo<u>n</u>

ANSWERPHONE MESSAGES

3 Listen to the messages on Philippe Sebald's answerphone and make a note of the days and times.

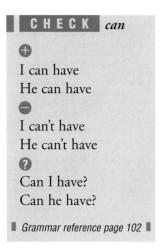

CHECK *can*

➕

I can have
He can have

➖

I can't have
He can't have

❓

Can I have?
Can he have?

Grammar reference page 102

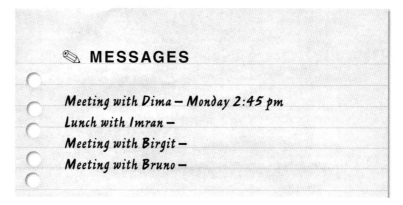

✎ **MESSAGES**

Meeting with Dima – Monday 2:45 pm
Lunch with Imran –
Meeting with Birgit –
Meeting with Bruno –

4 Look at the diary again. Which arrangements are possible and which arrangements are not possible? Write sentences with *can* and *can't*.

He can have a meeting with Dima at 2:45 on Monday afternoon.

A TELEPHONE ARRANGEMENT

5 Listen to the telephone conversation and answer these questions.

1 Look at the messages above again. Who does Philippe Sebald call?
2 What day and time do they arrange for their meeting?

6 Fill the gaps with the phrases in the box. Then listen again and check.

■ Hi. Bruno Ponzi.

○ Hello, Bruno. _____

■ Hey, Philippe. _____

○ Fine, thanks, fine. Bruno, _____
this meeting on Sunday. I'm sorry but
_____ then. I never work on
Sunday. How about Saturday?
_____ on Saturday afternoon?

■ Saturday afternoon's OK. Two o'clock?

○ _____ two fifteen?

■ Two fifteen's great. At the office?

○ Sure. _____

■ Great. See you.

I can't meet you
See you there.
It's Philippe here.
How are you?
Can we meet
it's about
Can you make it

NOW YOU

7 Role play two situations where you make arrangements.

▌ **A** Turn to page 94. **B** Turn to page 97 and call A.
▌ **B** Turn to page 97. **A** Turn to page 94 and call B.

real world *Telephoning*

STARTING A CALL   **1**   🎧   Listen to the phone conversation. Who are the two people?

a salesperson and a customer?
a manager and a secretary?
a teacher and a student?

2   🎧 👥   Match the phrases with similar meaning. Then listen again. Tick (✓) the phrases you hear in the conversation.

I'd like to speak to Alan.   Can you say that again?
Certainly.   Can you hold?
Can you repeat that?   Can I speak to Alan?
Just a moment.   Of course.

I'm afraid he's in a meeting.

MAKING EXCUSES   **3**   🎧   Next the secretary talks to Alan. Listen. What two excuses does Alan give for not speaking on the phone? Tick (✓) two of these sentences.

He's at lunch.   He's on another line.
He's in a meeting.   He's with a customer.

OBJECT PRONOUNS   **4**   Replace the names in brackets ( ) with an object pronoun.

1   Can you tell (Lisa) _____ I'm in a meeting.
2   I'd like to speak to (Alan) _____, please.
3   Can he meet (Lisa and me) _____ at three o'clock?
4   He's at lunch with (Fiona and Bill) _____ .
5   Can you leave (the car) _____ at the hotel?
6   Yes, it's Lisa. Can you ask (Alan) _____ to call (Lisa) _____ ?

CHECK	Object pronouns				
I	**me**	he	**him**	we	**us**
you	**you**	she	**her**	you	**you**
		it	**it**	they	**them**

LEAVING A MESSAGE

5 🎧 Listen to the rest of the phone conversation between the secretary and Lisa and answer these questions.

1 What excuse does the secretary give?

_____

2 What's Lisa's message?

_____

6 🎧 👥 Replace the <u>underlined</u> phrases below with these phrases from the conversation that you heard. Then listen again and check.

You're welcome.   **My number's**   **Can you tell him**   **I'm afraid that**

Would you like to leave   **And can you ask him to call me?**

- ■ Hello? <u>I'm sorry, but</u> Alan's with a customer at the moment. <u>Can I take</u> a message?
- ○ Yes. <u>Say that</u> it's Lisa. <u>And can he ring me?</u> <u>I'm on</u> 777 9876.
- ■ Certainly.
- ○ Thank you.
- ■ <u>Not at all.</u> Goodbye.

NOW YOU

7 👥 Take turns to play each role in this phone call, using the language on these pages.

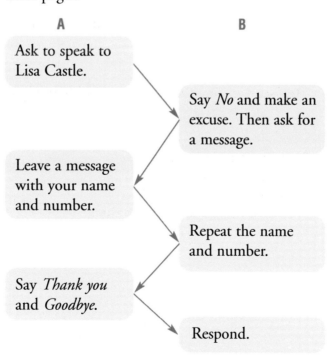

A

B

Ask to speak to Lisa Castle.

Say *No* and make an excuse. Then ask for a message.

Leave a message with your name and number.

Repeat the name and number.

Say *Thank you* and *Goodbye.*

Respond.

4 places

**THE LOYOLA LAW
SCHOOL**

1  Look at this picture of the Loyola Law School in Los Angeles, USA. Discuss your answers to the questions below.

*I think the buildings
are boring.*

*No, I think they're
really interesting.*

Are the buildings boring or interesting?   **Are they old or new?**

Is the street busy or quiet?   **Is it clean or dirty?**

Is the area safe or dangerous?   **Is it rich or poor?**

Is the car expensive or cheap?   **Is it fast or slow?**

Is the weather hot or cold?   **Is it sunny or dull?**

A LOYOLA STUDENT   **2** 🎧 👥 Listen to a student talking about the picture opposite. Then use some of the adjectives opposite to fill the gaps. Listen again and check.

The Loyola Law School? I love it. I think it's a really _____ building. I mean, it's _____ and it's beautiful. The street? It's nothing special. It's a _____ street, it's usually _____ . You know, it's a good area. It's not a _____ area, but it's _____ . And the car? Actually, that's my car. I always park there on Tuesdays. OK, it's not an _____ car, but it's very, very _____ . So, today's weather? Well, it's _____ and it's _____ . It's a good day to study, I guess.

SHORT CONVERSATIONS   **3** 👥 Use the adjectives opposite to fill the gaps.

1 Do you like New York?   Yes, it's a really *interesting* place.
2 How _____ is your boss?   He's about thirty-five.
3 There's a lot of money in Atlanta. Yes, it's a _____ city.
4 How _____ is your car?   Its top speed's about 200 km / hour.
5 This place isn't very _____ . No, there's rubbish everywhere.
6 The weather's good today, isn't it? Yes, it's very _____ and _____ .
7 Can I speak to you for a moment?   No, I'm sorry, I'm very _____ .
8 Is this _____ ?   No, it's only $5.

NOW YOU   **4** 👥 Use the adjectives on these pages to talk about these things in your life.

your area   **your building**   **your car**   **the weather today**   **your street**

My area's really boring.   *My building's very quiet.*

PRONUNCIATION   **A** 🎧 Listen and repeat. Notice the underlined vowel sounds.
/uː/ /ɑː/ /ɔː/

/uː/	/ɑː/	/ɔː/
sch<u>oo</u>l	c<u>a</u>r	sh<u>or</u>t
b<u>eau</u>tiful	<u>a</u>re	b<u>o</u>ring

B 🎧 Listen and repeat these phrases. Which vowel sounds in each phrase are the same?

Are y<u>ou</u> a st<u>u</u>dent?   Park your car here.   Do you like it?
New York Law School.

GRAMMAR Comparatives and superlatives

COMPARING PLACES 1 👥 How much do you know about the world? Discuss the questions in the quiz. Then turn to page 101 to find the answers.

> I think that New York is more expensive than Tokyo.

> I think Portugal has the safest drivers.

TRAVEL QUIZ

1 Where is life cheaper?
New York   Tokyo

2 Which of these cities has the most expensive taxis?
Cairo   Los Angeles   Paris

3 Which city is more dangerous?
Johannesburg   Rome

4 Where do you find the safest drivers in the world?
Argentina   Sweden   Portugal

5 Which city has worse pollution?
London   Reykjavik

6 Which of these cities has the worst traffic problems?
Bangkok   Riyadh   Vancouver

7 Which country has a better standard of living?
Ireland   Luxembourg

8 Which of these cities has the best beaches?
Belgrade   New Delhi   Rio de Janeiro

CHECK Comparatives and superlatives

Adjectives with one syllable, add *-er* for comparatives and *-est* for superlatives.
cheap   cheap**er than**   **the** cheap**est**

Adjectives with two or more syllables, put *more* or *most* before the adjective.
expensive   **more** expensive **than**   **the most** expensive

Some adjectives are irregular.
good   **better**   **best**   bad   **worse**   **worst**

▌ *Grammar reference page 103* ▌

**GOOD,
BETTER, BEST**

2 Use some of the words in the quiz opposite to complete this table.

ADJECTIVE	COMPARATIVE	SUPERLATIVE
good		
bad		
expensive	more expensive	
cheap		cheapest
dangerous		most dangerous
safe	safer	

COUNTRY FACTS

3 Fill the gaps in the sentences with the superlative form of these adjectives.

long   small   dangerous   cold   popular

1 People in Santiago, Chile, work the _____ hours in the world: more than 2,000 hours a year.
2 Oymyakon in Siberia is the _____ town in the world. Temperatures can go down to around −65°C.
3 Vatican City is the world's _____ country. Around 1,000 people live there.
4 France is the world's _____ country for a holiday. It gets about 70 million tourists a year.
5 Statistics say that your home is the _____ place in the world. That's where most accidents happen!

4 Use these prompts to write questions using comparatives. Then take turns to ask and answer them.

1 Siberia / cold / Norway   *Is Siberia colder than Norway?*
2 Spain / popular with tourists / France   _____
3 working hours in Chile / long / in Germany _____
4 Madagascar / small / Vatican City   _____
5 your home / dangerous / the city streets _____

NOW YOU

5 Use the language on these pages to compare your country or city with other countries or cities that you know.

working life *Directions*

GIVING DIRECTIONS **1** 👥 Match the directions to the signs.

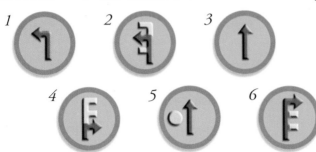

Turn left.

Take the first turning on your right.

Go past . . .

Take the second turning on your left.

Go straight . . .

Take the third turning on your right.

A MEETING IN RIO **2** 👥 Read this e-mail. Look at the map opposite. Find the hotel and then follow Mois's route. Fill the boxes on the map with these words.

gym   obelisk   country club

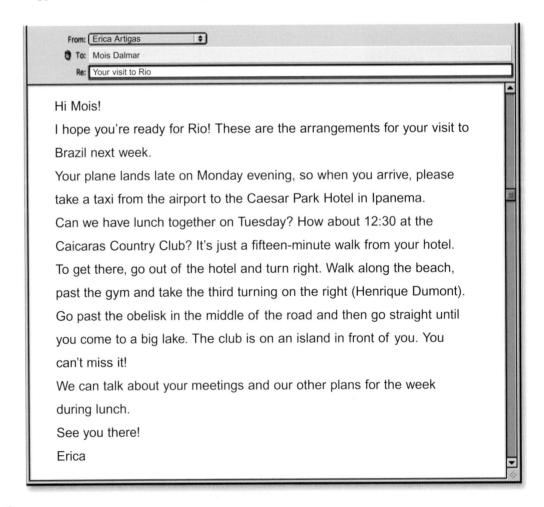

From: Erica Artigas
To: Mois Dalmar
Re: Your visit to Rio

Hi Mois!

I hope you're ready for Rio! These are the arrangements for your visit to Brazil next week.

Your plane lands late on Monday evening, so when you arrive, please take a taxi from the airport to the Caesar Park Hotel in Ipanema.

Can we have lunch together on Tuesday? How about 12:30 at the Caicaras Country Club? It's just a fifteen-minute walk from your hotel. To get there, go out of the hotel and turn right. Walk along the beach, past the gym and take the third turning on the right (Henrique Dumont). Go past the obelisk in the middle of the road and then go straight until you come to a big lake. The club is on an island in front of you. You can't miss it!

We can talk about your meetings and our other plans for the week during lunch.

See you there!

Erica

3 🎧 Listen to the voicemail that Mois gets when he arrives in Brazil. What time is his meeting now? And where is it? Follow the route on the map.

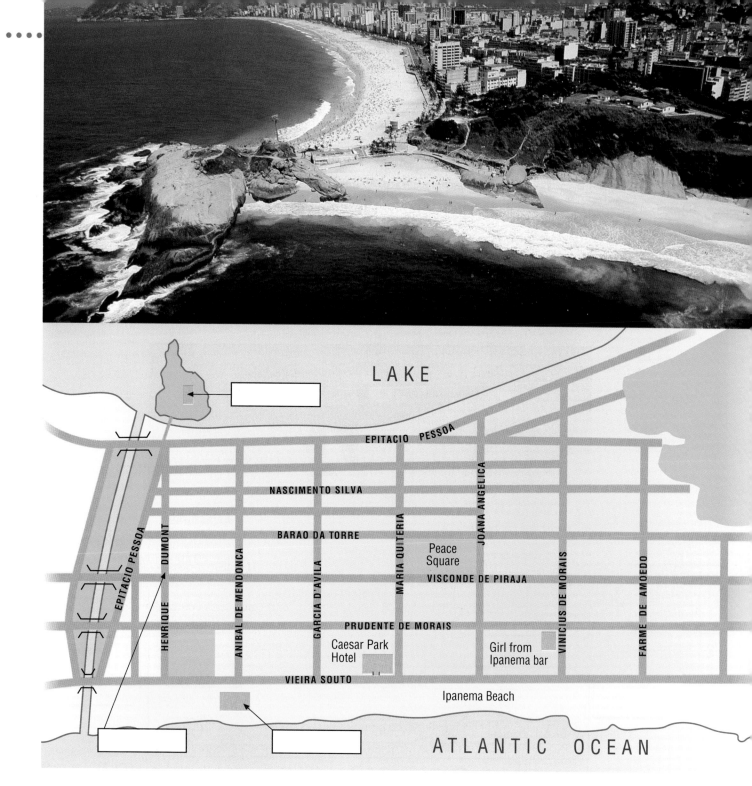

LAKE

EPITACIO PESSOA

NASCIMENTO SILVA

BARAO DA TORRE

EPITACIO PESSOA

HENRIQUE DUMONT

ANIBAL DE MENDONCA

GARCIA D'AVILA

MARIA QUITERIA

JOANA ANGELICA

Peace
Square

VISCONDE DE PIRAJA

VINICIUS DE MORAIS

FARME DE AMOEDO

PRUDENTE DE MORAIS

Caesar Park
Hotel

Girl from
Ipanema bar

VIEIRA SOUTO

Ipanema Beach

ATLANTIC OCEAN

NOW YOU **4** Take turns to give directions on the map above.

▌**A** Turn to page 95 and give B directions.
  B Start at the country club – where do you go?
▌**B** Turn to page 98 and give A directions.
  A Start at the gym on the beach – where do you go?

5 Write an e-mail that gives directions for one of the following:

▌ how to get from your home to a shop or supermarket
▌ how to get from your workplace to a restaurant near you

real world *Hotels*

A HOTEL WEBSITE   **1** Look at the website. Where do you click to find out about these things? Write the words in the right boxes.

room service   fax machines   swimming pool
luxury suites   sauna   gym   good transport links
city centre location   good food   meeting rooms
Internet access   conference rooms   cheap prices

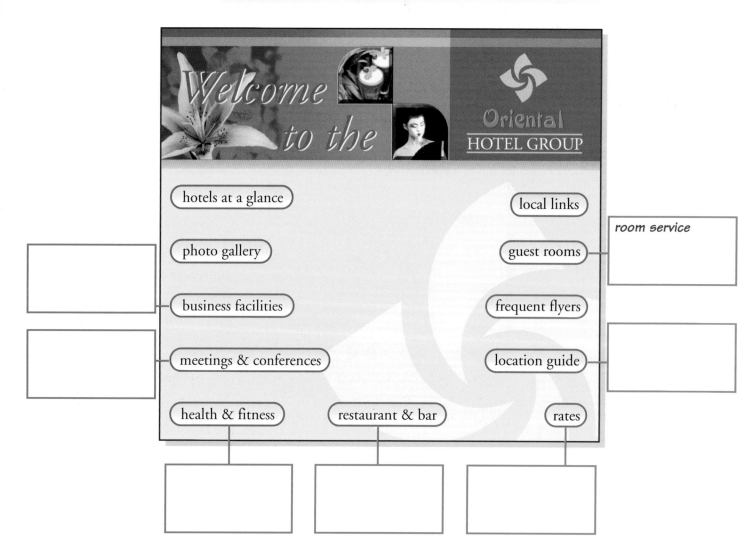

Welcome to the Oriental HOTEL GROUP

hotels at a glance

photo gallery

business facilities

meetings & conferences

health & fitness   restaurant & bar

local links

guest rooms → room service

frequent flyers

location guide

rates

2 Which of the facilities above do you think are important in a good business hotel? List your top five.

I think the most important thing is a swimming pool.

No, I think conference rooms are more important.

COMPARING HOTELS **3** 🎧 👥 Listen to descriptions of three of the world's most famous hotels and take notes. Then work together to make a list of facilities for each one. Listen again and check.

The Oriental, Bangkok

Ice Hotel

Chelsea Hotel

Oriental: conf. rooms

NOW YOU **4** 👥 Now talk about these questions.

1 Which hotel do you think is the best for a holiday? Why?
2 Which hotel do you think is the best for a big business meeting? Why?
3 Which hotel do you think is the most interesting? Why?

I think the Chelsea Hotel is the best for a holiday.

Why?

Because it's in a city centre.

PRONUNCIATION 🎧 Listen and repeat these phrases. Concentrate on the /l/ and /r/ sounds.
/l/ /r/ room rates   health club   hotel restaurant   Chelsea Hotel
luxury location   transport links   conference rooms

review 2

VOCABULARY
Crossword

1 Complete this crossword with words from Units 3 and 4.

Across ▶

1 This is clue number one, so it's the _____ clue. (5)

3 6:30 = _____ past six (4)

6 What's your job? = What _____ you do? (2)

9 The opposite of *boring*. (11)

10 Is this the train _____ San Jose? (2)

11 Never = 0% _____ = 100% (6)

12 The superlative of *bad*. (5)

14 Another word for hotel *prices*. (5)

16 The opposite of *dull* weather. (5)

17 Can I _____ a message, please? (5)

Down ▼

2 A person who sells. (11)

4 A person who works in a shop is a shop _____ . (9)

5 Singapore Airlines has a lot of _____ every day. (7)

6 The opposite of *clean*. (5)

7 The meeting is _____ Thursday. (2)

8 Can you say it again? = Can you _____ it? (6)

13 I – my, you – your, he – _____ (3)

15 Goodbye. _____ you tomorrow. (3)

GRAMMAR CHECK

2 Put the verbs in brackets ( ) into the correct form of the present simple.

1 Where (you live) _____ ?
   I (live) _____ in Cairo.
2 What (she do) _____ ?
   She (work) _____ for a big company.
3 Where (they come) _____ from?
   I (not know) _____ !
4 When (he go) _____ to the office?
   He (go) _____ to the office at 8 o'clock.
5 What excuse (the secretary give) _____ ?
   She (say) _____ he's in a meeting.
6 Where (people work) _____ the longest hours?
   They (work) _____ the longest hours in Chile.

3 Complete this table.

ADJECTIVE	good		expensive		
COMPARATIVE		worse			faster
SUPERLATIVE	best			dirtiest	

FOCUS ON ...
Prepositions of
movement

4 🎧 Write these prepositions under the correct arrow. Then listen and check.

out of   into   round   along   across   up   down   through

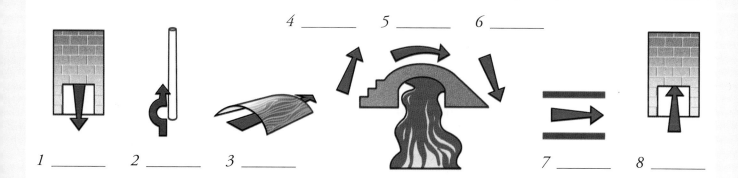

4 _____   5 _____   6 _____

1 _____   2 _____   3 _____   7 _____   8 _____

PRONUNCIATION
/g/ /k/

A 🎧 Listen and repeat. Notice the underlined sounds.

/g/   /k/
<u>g</u>et   <u>c</u>all
<u>g</u>uide   <u>q</u>uiet

B 🎧 Say these pairs of words. Then listen and tick (✓) the word from each pair that you hear.

good   could   gold   cold   bang   bank

5 speed and power

TRAVEL IN DUBAI

1 👥 Look at the pictures of Dubai on these pages. What kinds of transport can you see? Put a tick (✓) or a cross (✗) next to these words.

bicycle	**bus**	**camel**	**car**	**helicopter**
motorbike	**plane**	**boat**	**taxi**	**train**

2 👥 Which of these sentences about the pictures is true?

There's a helicopter.
There are some buses.
There aren't any camels.

3 Write sentences about the other kinds of transport in the box above.

There's a …   There are some …   There aren't any …

CHECK	*there is … there are …*			
	➕	➖	❓	**Short answers**
Singular	There's a car.	There isn't a car.	Is there a car?	Yes, there is.
Plural	There are **some** cars.	There aren't **any** cars.	Are there **any** cars?	No, there aren't.

A TRAVEL REPORT **4** 🎧 👥 Read and listen to this travel report about Dubai. Circle the correct word or phrase in *italics*. Then listen again and check.

Dubai

For tourists and businesspeople, Dubai is one of the most popular places in the Middle East. There are *a / some* fantastic facilities for businesspeople and, for tourists, there are *a lot of / any* great hotels, beaches and shops.

Transport in Dubai is not a problem. There's *a / some* big new airport, there are *a lot of / a* taxis and there are also *any / some* buses. But I'm afraid there aren't *any / some* trains and, of course, there aren't *a / any* bicycles, because it's very, very hot!

But in this city, there's really only one way to travel – the car. People in Dubai love their cars. And there's *a / a lot of* good reason for this: petrol here is very cheap. So, there are always *a lot of / any* cars on the streets and there are *any / some* very noisy motorbikes, too!

And for people who want the old Dubai, there are still *some / a* camels here!

Travel report

CHECK *there is … there are …*

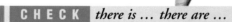

There aren't any boats.

There's a boat.

There are some boats.

There are a lot of boats.

NOW YOU **5** 👥 Use the language on these pages to talk about transport in your town or city.

> *In my city, there are a lot of bicycles.*

> *There aren't any trains in my town.*

GRAMMAR Countable and uncountable nouns

CAN YOU MATCH THEM?

1 👥 Match these words to the words in the pictures.

power station   information   money

barrels   rooms   bottle   factory   space

stars _____

pollution _____

electricity
power station

dollars _____

water _____

oil _____

newspapers _____

accommodation _____

CAN YOU COUNT THEM?

2 Look at the pairs of words opposite. In each pair, which word is countable and which word is uncountable? Write the words in the correct group.

COUNTABLE	*dollars*				
UNCOUNTABLE	*money*				

CHECK Countable and uncountable nouns

Dollars are countable, because you can say *two dollars*.
Money is uncountable because you can't say ~~two moneys.~~

▎ *Grammar reference page 104* ▎

**THERE IS ...
THERE ARE ...**

3 Complete these sentences. Use *There are …* for countable nouns and *There is …* for uncountable nouns.

1 *There are* ____ some bottles of water on the table.
2 _____ a lot of oil under the sea.
3 _____ a lot of power stations in Russia.
4 _____ some English language newspapers in Singapore.
5 _____ a lot of information on the Internet.
6 _____ a lot of film stars in Hollywood.

NOW YOU

4 Take turns to ask questions about these things. Reply using short answers.
a lot of cars in Egypt?
a lot of space in Australia?
a lot of shops in Paris?
a lot of water in Saudi Arabia?
any electricity in space?
any cheap accommodation in Tokyo?

> Are there a lot of cars in Egypt?

> Yes, there are.

5 Think of five more questions to ask another pair.

PRONUNCIATION
/s/ /t/ /ʃ/

A Listen and repeat. Notice the underlined sounds.

/s/	/t/	/ʃ/
<u>s</u>tar <u>sp</u>a<u>c</u>e	<u>T</u>okyo In<u>t</u>erne<u>t</u>	<u>sh</u>op informa<u>t</u>ion

B Listen to the underlined sounds in these words. Put the words in one of the three groups above.

Ru<u>ss</u>ia   <u>s</u>ea   accommoda<u>t</u>ion   <u>S</u>ingapore   bo<u>tt</u>le   wa<u>t</u>er
electri<u>c</u>ity   Engli<u>sh</u>   lo<u>t</u>

working **life** *Talking about companies*

QUESTIONS ABOUT COMPANIES

1 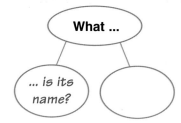 Match these phrases to the question words below.

is its name?   are its big markets?
is its head office?   is its boss?
does it make?   are its main competitors?

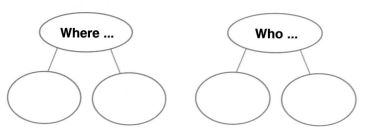

2 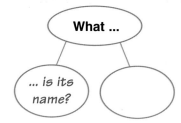 Read the information on this website and then take turns to ask and answer the questions above.

PH
Company *Check* ✓

(Company profile) (Sales report) (Products) (Financial analysis)

Company information: Vestas

Vestas Wind Systems A/S is a big producer of wind turbines.
(These are machines that produce electricity from the wind.)

Some Vestas turbines cost more than $1 million, but they produce very cheap electricity. They're also quiet and they don't produce any pollution.

The company sells a lot of its wind turbines in Europe, especially in countries like Denmark, Spain and Germany, but they also have big markets in India and the USA. In fact there are now more than 7,000 Vestas wind turbines in about thirty-five countries.

The company's boss, J Poulsen, manages the business from the head office in Ringkobing, Denmark, but Vestas has more than 4,000 employees in its factories and offices around the world.

The financial position of the company is good. It makes a profit of around 10 per cent on its total sales. However, there are some strong competitors in this market, including NEG Micon A/S (Denmark) and Babcock Borsig AG (Germany).

Home   Company profile   Sales report   Products   Financial analysis

STATISTICS

3 👥 Look at the website again. Are these sentences true (T) or false (F)?

CHECK

more than a thousand	>1,000
less than a thousand	<1,000
around/about a thousand	≈1,000

1 Vestas turbines cost more than one million dollars.
2 There are around five thousand five hundred Vestas turbines in the world.
3 There are Vestas turbines in more than a hundred countries.
4 Vestas has less than four thousand employees.
5 Vestas makes a profit of about five per cent on its total sales.

HOW MUCH?
HOW MANY?

4 Use these prompts to write questions with *How much* or *How many*, putting the verbs in brackets ( ) into the correct form.

1 turbines / the company (sell) in Europe
How many turbines does the company sell in Europe?

2 profit / the company (make)
_____

3 pollution / the turbines (produce)
_____

4 employees / the company (have)
_____

5 turbines / (be) there in the world
_____

6 money / a wind turbine (cost)
_____

5 👥 Take turns to ask and answer your questions.

CHECK	*How much … ?* and *How many … ?*

How much … ? is used for things you can't count.
How many … ? is used for things you can count.

❚ Grammar reference page 104 ❚

NOW YOU

6 Write some sentences about your company (or a company that you know), using some of the language on these pages.

7 👥 Use the questions on these pages to find out about your partner's company. Make notes and check the spelling of any unknown words. Then swap roles.

Where's your head office?   Can you spell that, please?

8 Write a short summary of your partner's company for a web page.

real world

Slowing down

LEISURE TIME IN THE USA

1 Look at the results of a survey about leisure time in the USA. Find the leisure activities that match the pictures on these pages.

The 10 most popular
Leisure Activities
in the USA

1 Reading
2 Watching TV
3 Spending time with the family
4 Working in the garden
5 Going fishing

6 Walking
7 Going to the movies
8 Using a computer
9 Socialising with friends
10 Going to the gym or playing sports

(Source: Harris Poll)

2 What are your three favourite leisure activities? Choose from the list above or use a dictionary to help you. Write three sentences.

I like watching TV.

CHECK *I like …*

I like + verb *-ing*
⊕ I like walking.
⊖ I don't like walking.
❓ Do you like walking?

---

3 Take turns to ask and answer these questions.

> What do you like doing in your free time?

> I like going to the movies.

> How often do you go to the movies?

> I go twice a week.

CHECK *How often?*

×1 once
×2 twice
×3 three times
×4 four times …

LEISURE TIME IN THE UK

4 🎧 👥 Listen to a conversation between a researcher and a British worker and fill the gaps.

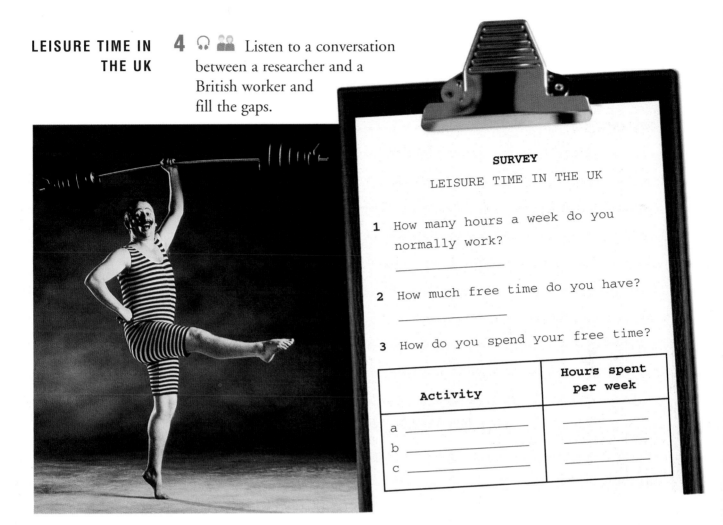

SURVEY

LEISURE TIME IN THE UK

1 How many hours a week do you normally work?

_____

2 How much free time do you have?

_____

3 How do you spend your free time?

Activity	Hours spent per week
a _____	_____
b _____	_____
c _____	_____

5 👥 Take turns to ask and answer the questions above with information about your life.

How do you spend your free time?

I spend about 8 hours a week watching TV.

CHECK *I spend …*

I spend + time + verb *-ing*
I spend 40 hours a week working.

NOW YOU

6 👥 Work together and write a questionnaire about leisure time. Write four or more questions. (Use the questions on these pages or make up others.) Then go around the class and make notes about other people's answers. What are the five most popular leisure activities in the class?

PRONUNCIATION /n/ /ŋ/

🎧 Listen and repeat these phrases. Concentrate on the /n/ and /ŋ/ sounds at the ends of the words.

slow<u>ing</u> dow<u>n</u>   watch<u>ing</u> televisio<u>n</u>   hav<u>ing</u> fu<u>n</u>   work<u>ing</u> in the garde<u>n</u>

6 business and pleasure

COUNTRIES AND CITIES

1 👥 Look at the world map and find cities from these countries.

Brazil _São Paulo_   Morocco _____
China _____   Pakistan _____
France _____   Russia _____
Japan _____   USA _____

AROUND THE WORLD

2 🎧 Listen to eight reports from cities around the world. As you listen, write the time next to cities 1–8.

3 What is happening at the moment? Fill the gaps in sentences 1–4 with these verbs.

> **coming   rising   having**
> **starting   getting**

4 Put these verbs into the *-ing* form. Then fill the gaps in sentences 5–8 to show what is happening now.

> **close   relax   get**
> **set   work   leave**

5 🎧 Listen again and check.

NOW YOU

6 👥 Talk about other places in the world. Say what the time is at the moment and talk about what people are doing.

> *1* New York _7 am_____
> The sun's _coming_ up
> and we're _____
> ready for the day.

> *2* São Paulo _____
> Everyone's _____ work.

midnight

am

am

am

am

3 **Casablanca** _____
  The temperature is _____ .

4 **Paris** _____
  We're _____ lunch.

5 **Moscow** _____
  It's _____ cold.

| C H E C K | Present continuous |

I am + verb *-ing*   *I am starting.*
You are + verb *-ing*   *You are working.*

We use the present continuous for things that
are happening now. *I'm learning English.*

❚ *Grammar reference page 105* ❚

7 **Beijing** _____
  The sun is _____ and everyone's
  _____ at the end of the day.

6 **Karachi** _____
  The stock market is
  _____ and people are
  _____ their offices.

8 **Tokyo** _____
  We're still _____ !

Noon   pm   pm   pm   pm   pm

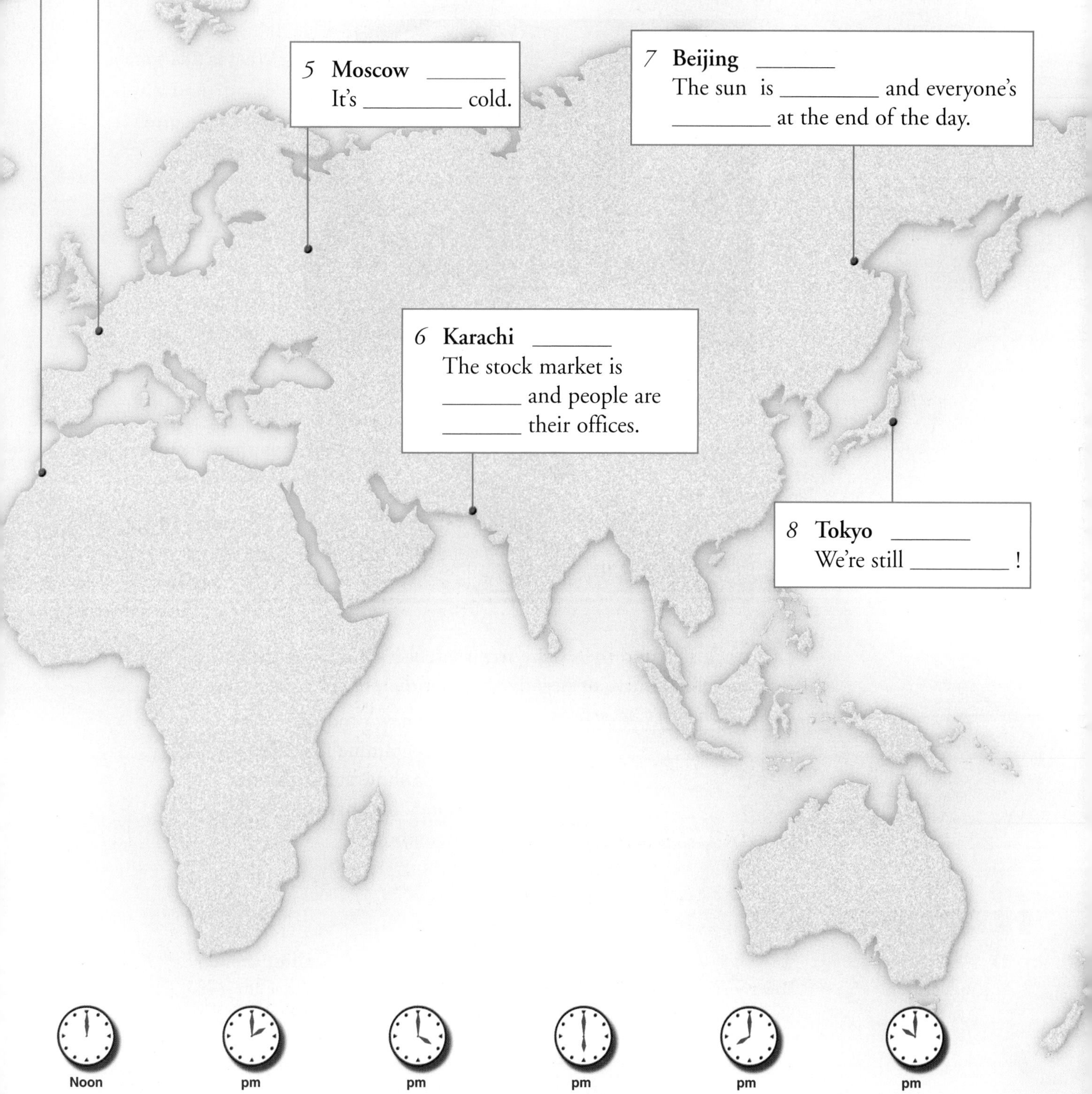

G R A M M A R Present continuous

WHAT'S SHE DOING?   **1** Look at this picture and talk about the questions.

> *I think she's making a programme for children's TV.*

> *No, I think she's …*

What is this woman doing? And why is she wearing a giraffe costume?

Is she advertising a new product?

Is she making a programme for children's TV?

Is she appearing in a show at the theatre?

Is she raising money for charity?

Or is she running a marathon?

2 Listen and then write true sentences by putting the verbs in brackets ( ) into the positive or negative form of the present continuous.

1 <u>She isn't advertising</u> (advertise) a new product.
2 _____ (make) a programme for children's TV.
3 _____ (appear) in a show at the theatre.
4 _____ (raise) money for charity.
5 _____ (run) a marathon.

C H E C K Present continuous			
➕	➖	❓	**Short answers**
You're working.	You aren't working.	Are you working?	Yes, I am. / No, I'm not.
She's working.	She isn't working.	Is she working?	Yes, she is. / No, she isn't.

▌ *Grammar reference page 105* ▌

SIMPLE OR CONTINUOUS?

3 🎧 Match the questions and answers. Then listen again and check.

What does she do?   She comes from Wales.
What is she doing?   She's wearing a funny costume.
Where does she come from?   She works as an administrator.
What is she wearing?   She's running a marathon.

4 👥 Look at the questions and answers above again. Which questions and answers are about the following?

1 something that's happening now
2 something that's usually true

> **CHECK** **Present simple or continuous?**
>
> We use the present continuous for things that are happening now.
> *She's running a marathon.*   *She's wearing a costume.*
>
> We use the present simple for things that are always or usually true.
> *She comes from Wales.*   *She works as an administrator.*
>
> ▮ *Grammar reference page 105* ▮

5 Here are some more sentences that you heard. Put the verbs in brackets ( ) into the present simple or the present continuous.

1 She (run) _____ the marathon every year.
2 She (smile) _____ at the camera.
3 She (feel) _____ very tired at the moment.
5 The marathon usually (take) _____ her more than seven hours.

NOW YOU

6 👥 Who are these people? Take turns to ask and answer questions.

▮ **A** Use the prompts below to ask questions about the person on the left.
  B Turn to page 98 and answer.

▮ **B** Use the prompts below to ask questions about the person on the right.
  A Turn to page 95 and answer.

What / do in the picture?
What / usually do?
What / wear in the picture?
Where / live?

working **life** *Shopping*

BAD SERVICE

1 🎧 Listen to a conversation between a customer and an assistant in a sports shop. Which of these adjectives describe the assistant?

polite   impolite   friendly   unfriendly   helpful   unhelpful

2 👥 What does the shop assistant do wrong? Discuss.

> *He isn't very polite.*

> *He says the manager's an idiot.*

3 👥 🎧 Look at what the customer (■) says in the conversation and circle the correct form of the verbs in *italics*. Then listen again and check.

■ Good morning.

○ _____

■ *I look for / I'm looking for* a wetsuit.

○ _____

■ But *it says / it's saying* in the window that you sell wetsuits.

○ _____

■ Oh … I see. Well, *do you sell / are you selling* surfboards?

○ _____

■ What? *Do you joke? / Are you joking?* This shop is Surfer's Paradise, right? And you're telling me that you *don't sell / aren't selling* surfboards.

○ _____

■ *I see / I'm seeing.* Well, where can I buy a surfboard?

○ _____

■ Right. Well, thank you very much. Goodbye.

○ _____

BETTER SERVICE

4 🎧 Now the customer is in the same situation but he is talking to a more polite shop assistant. Fill the gaps in the conversation opposite with these sentences. Then listen to the new conversation and check.

> **Yes. I'm afraid that sign's a mistake.**   **Goodbye. Have a nice day.**
> **No, I'm afraid we don't.**   **I'm sorry, but we don't sell wetsuits.**
> **Why don't you try the shop across the road?**   **Hello. Can I help you?**
> **Yes, I know it's crazy, but we're having problems with our supplier.**

5 👥 Read the conversation that you've written opposite.

SHOPPING PHRASES

6 🎧 You are looking for some clothes. Write these phrases next to the four steps below. Then listen to the customer's next conversation and check.

> **Can I have a receipt?**   **Can I try them on?**
> **Can I pay by credit card?**   **Can I have this one?**

You want to check the size.   _____
↓
You make your decision.   _____
↓
You don't have any cash.   _____
↓
You want a record of the price.   _____

NOW YOU

7 👥 Use the language on these pages to role play these situations.

▌**A** You want to buy a sports bag and some running shoes. Turn to page 95.
  B You work in a shop. Turn to page 98.

▌**B** You want to buy a tennis racquet. Turn to page 98.
  A You work in a shop. Turn to page 95.

PRONUNCIATION
/æ/ /aɪ/ /ə/ /ʊ/

A 🎧 Listen and repeat these words. Notice the differences between the underlined sounds.

/æ/	/aɪ/	/ə/	/ʊ/
c<u>a</u>sh	n<u>i</u>ce	th<u>e</u>	g<u>oo</u>d
<u>a</u>nd	tr<u>y</u>	<u>a</u>fraid	l<u>oo</u>k

B 🎧 Listen to the underlined sounds in these words and put them in one of the four groups above.

<u>a</u>cross   r<u>a</u>cquet   b<u>a</u>d   r<u>igh</u>t   b<u>uy</u>   s<u>ig</u>n   m<u>a</u>nager
s<u>u</u>pplier   p<u>o</u>lite   w<u>o</u>man   p<u>u</u>t

real world

Networking

MEETING PEOPLE **1** Compare your answers to these questions.

1 In business life, which do you think is more important?
what you know   who you know

2 Where do you meet new people?
at conferences   at parties   I never meet new people.

3 How many names do you have in your address book?
less than 20   21 to 50   51 to 100   more than 100

2 Read this text and answer the questions opposite.

The queen of 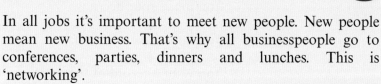 networking

In all jobs it's important to meet new people. New people mean new business. That's why all businesspeople go to conferences, parties, dinners and lunches. This is 'networking'.

But how can you be good at networking? Just ask Carole Stone!

Carole Stone is London's networking queen. She has more than 14,000 names in her address book. Every year she has a party for 1,400 people. Her friends are top businesspeople, politicians and film stars.

How does she do it? In her book, *Networking*, she writes about the secrets of her success with people. Here is some of her advice.

- Always carry lots of your business cards with you.
- Ask people lots of questions. (Before a meeting or a party, think of questions that start with *How … ?* and *What … ?*)
- When you speak to new people, never talk about your problems.
- After a meeting or a party, write notes about the new people and your conversations.
- Always send a thank-you letter or e-mail after a party, dinner or lunch.
- Always spell people's names correctly when you write to them.

NETWORKING
ADVICE

1 How many names does Carole Stone have in her address book?
2 What kind of people are her friends?
3 What's the name of her book?
4 Look at her advice. Which of the things do you do …
… always? … sometimes? … never?

> *I never make notes after a party.*

> *I always spell people's names correctly.*

QUESTION WORDS

3 Look at the questions and answers about the text opposite. Fill the gaps with these question words.

How many   How   What   Why   Where

1 _____ do businesspeople go to conferences?
Because they want to meet people.
2 _____ can you be good at networking?
Just ask Carole Stone!
3 _____'s Carole Stone from?
London.
4 _____ people go to her parties?
1,400
5 _____ do you send after a party, dinner or lunch?
A thank-you letter or e-mail.

ASKING QUESTIONS

4 Match the questions with similar meanings.

Where do you come from?   Where's your home?
Where do you live?   Where are you from?
Who do you work for?   Who are you?
What do you do?   What's the name of your company?
What's your name?   What's your job?

NOW YOU

5 Network with other people in the class. Use Carole Stone's advice: ask lots of questions. Then write some notes about the people.

review 3

VOCABULARY
Collocations

1 Which words go together? Look at Units 5 and 6 to help you.

tennis	office	_tennis racquet_
head	station	_____
film	service	_____
address	racquet	_____
credit	turbine	_____
customer	book	_____
power	card	_____
wind	star	_____

2 Which verbs and nouns go together?

watch	a marathon	_watch TV_
spend	TV	_____
play	fishing	_____
go	time	_____
run	sports	_____

GRAMMAR CHECK

3 Fill the gaps with *How much* or *How many*.

1 _____ information do you have?
2 _____ space is there on the first floor?
3 _____ stars can you see?
4 _____ bottles are there on the table?
5 _____ accommodation is there in the city centre?

4 Decide whether these sentences are about something which usually happens or something which is happening now. Then put the verbs in brackets ( ) into the correct form of the present simple or the present continuous.

1 Don't speak to them – they (work) _____ .
2 She (arrive) _____ at the office at 9:30 every day.
3 I (look) _____ for a computer – but not an expensive one.
4 He can't come to the phone because he (have) _____ a meeting.
5 What (your company produce) _____ ?
6 Why (he look) _____ out of the window?

FOCUS ON ...
Adverbs

5 Read this report about an employee. Then use the underlined adverbs to complete the table.

Summary

Manfred is one of our
best employees. He works
well under pressure,
because he thinks
clearly. He usually finds
solutions to problems
quickly and efficiently.
He is also very good
with customers: he talks
to them politely and
listens carefully.

ADJECTIVE	ADVERB
careful	*carefully*
clear	
efficient	
good	
polite	
quick	
usual	

6 Fill the gaps in these sentences with some of the adverbs in the table.

1 The roads are very busy today, so drive _____ .

2 She _____ arrives at 9:30.

3 I understand her very well, because she explains things _____ .

4 It's not a problem because he's working very _____ today.

PRONUNCIATION
/ʃ/ and /tʃ/ /ʒ/ and /dʒ/

A ◌ Listen and repeat. Notice the underlined sounds.

/ʃ/	/tʃ/
shop	cheap
conversation	check
machine	watch

B ◌ Listen and repeat these phrases. Concentrate on the /ʃ/ and /tʃ/ sounds.

children's show   charity shop   how much cash?   fish for lunch

C ◌ Listen and repeat. Notice the underlined sounds.

/ʒ/	/dʒ/
pleasure	joke
usually	Germany

D ◌ Listen to the underlined sounds in these words. Put the words in one of the two groups above.

giraffe   television   decision   job

7 technology

BUSINESS FIRSTS **1** 👥 Put these events in the history of business in the correct order.

☐ the first TV advert

☐ the first tourist in space

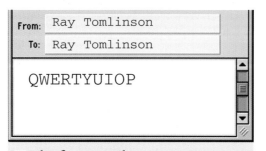

From: Ray Tomlinson
To: Ray Tomlinson

QWERTYUIOP

☐ the first e-mail

☐ the first passenger flight

☐ the first phone call

DATES

CHECK Months	
January	July
February	August
March	September
April	October
May	November
June	December

* = 3/10/1875 in US English (month before day)

2 Write these dates as figures.

1 the tenth of March eighteen seventy-five   *10/3/1875* *
2 nineteen seventy-one   _____
3 July the first nineteen forty-one   _____
4 the twenty-eighth of April two thousand and one   _____
5 January the first nineteen fourteen   _____

3 Match the dates to the events opposite. Then turn to page 101 to find out if you're right.

THE FIRST E-MAIL

4 Listen to the story of the first e-mail. Then read the text and circle the correct form of *to be*.

The American computer scientist, Ray Tomlinson, *was / were* the first person to send an e-mail. It *was / were* some time in 1971, but he can't remember exactly when. It *wasn't / weren't* big news at the time because the two computers *was / were* in the same room. And his message *wasn't / weren't* very interesting – it *was / were* just: 'QWERTYUIOP'. Why? *Was / Were* this a new computer language? No, they *was / were* the letters at the top of his computer's keyboard!

5 Fill the gaps with *was* or *were*. Then take turns to ask and answer the questions.

1 When *was* the first e-mail?
2 _____ it big news?
3 Where _____ the two computers?
4 What _____ the message?
5 Where _____ the letters of the message?

CHECK The past of *to be*

⊕	⊖	❓	Short answers
He was the first.	He wasn't the first.	Was he the first?	Yes, he was. / No, he wasn't.
They were the first.	They weren't the first.	Were they the first?	Yes, they were. / No, they weren't.

Grammar reference page 105

NOW YOU

6 Ask and answer some more questions about business firsts.
A Turn to page 95. **B** Turn to page 98.

When was the first … ?   It was …

GRAMMAR Past simple (1)

REGULAR VERBS

1 Read the story of the first TV advert and write the past form of these verbs.

appear	*appeared*	disappear	_____	watch	_____
stay	_____	ask	_____	interrupt	_____

The first TV advert

On the evening of 1 July 1941, a lot of New Yorkers were at home to watch the baseball game on TV between the New York Dodgers and the Philadelphia Phillies. But that evening they watched more than just a baseball game; they also watched a small piece of business history.

Because at one point in the evening, the TV station interrupted the programme and a Bulova watch appeared on the screen. It stayed there for sixty seconds and then disappeared.

'What was that?' people asked. In fact, it was the world's first TV advert!

2 🎧 Listen to the story of the first phone call. Then fill the gaps with the past form of these verbs. (They're all regular.)

laugh   call   realise   ask   show   start

The first phone call

The first phone call was on March 10 1875, when Alexander Graham Bell, the inventor of the telephone, _____ his assistant. His first words were, 'Mr Watson, come here, I want you.'

Bell and Watson _____ that their phone was a fantastic business idea. They _____ it to some American businessmen and _____ for $100,000. But the businessmen _____: 'It's just an electrical toy.'

So Bell _____ his own company and soon, with the name American Telephone and Telegraph, it was the top company in the USA.

CHECK	Regular past verbs				
Present		Past	Present		Past
appear	+-*ed*	appear**ed**	start	+-*ed*	start**ed**
ask	+-*ed*	ask**ed**	show	+-*ed*	show**ed**

▌ Grammar reference page 104 ▌

IRREGULAR VERBS **3** 👥 Read the story and write the past form of these verbs. (They don't end in *-ed* because they're irregular.)

leave *left*   go _____   have _____
fly _____   cost _____   make _____

The first passenger flight
The first passenger flight left from St Petersburg, Florida on 1 January 1914 and went to Tampa Bay, less than 40 kilometres away. It was a very small plane and it only had space for the pilot and one passenger.
  For the next four months, the plane flew between St Petersburg and Tampa Bay two times a day, and a return ticket cost $10. This first airline company only made a very small profit, but it was the start of a very big industry!

CHECK Irregular past verbs

Present	Past	Present	Past	Present	Past
be	→ was/were	do	→ did	make	→ made
go	→ went	have	→ had	cost	→ cost

For more, go to page 120

REGULAR AND IRREGULAR **4** 🎧 👥 Read this story and put the verbs in brackets ( ) into the correct form. (Some are regular and some are irregular.) Then listen and check.

The first tourist in space
For many years Dennis Tito (be) _____ a top American businessman. During his career, he (make) _____ millions and millions of dollars. But he always (have) _____ a dream – to be an astronaut. So, one day, he (ask) _____ the American space agency NASA, 'How much does it cost to go into space?' The answer (be) _____ : 'Sorry. Space is not for tourists.'
So, Tito (go) _____ to the Russians and (ask) _____ them the same question. The Russians (be not) _____ sure. 'How about $20 million?' (ask) _____ Tito. This time, the answer (be) _____ 'Yes'.
And so in April 2001, Tito (leave) _____ from Baikonur, Kazakhstan in a Russian Soyuz-TM rocket and (fly) _____ to the International Space Station. While he (be) _____ in space, Tito (have) _____ a fantastic time, just like a normal tourist!

NOW YOU **5** 👥 Work in groups. Group **A** Turn to page 95. Group **B** Turn to page 98. Take turns to tell one of the stories to each other.

working life *Computer problems*

E-MAIL **1** 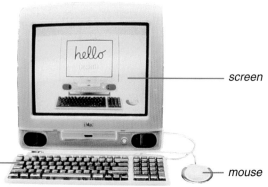 Tamara Vela works from home. She has a problem with her computer and e-mails her friend, Alex. Quickly read the e-mail below and find the answers to these questions.

1 Which part of her computer has a problem?
2 How old is her computer?
3 How can Alex contact her?
4 Her computer isn't working, so how can she send e-mails?

screen

keyboard

mouse

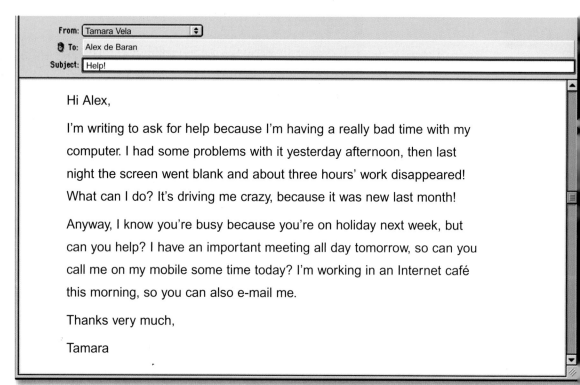

From: Tamara Vela

To: Alex de Baran

Subject: Help!

Hi Alex,

I'm writing to ask for help because I'm having a really bad time with my computer. I had some problems with it yesterday afternoon, then last night the screen went blank and about three hours' work disappeared! What can I do? It's driving me crazy, because it was new last month!

Anyway, I know you're busy because you're on holiday next week, but can you help? I have an important meeting all day tomorrow, so can you call me on my mobile some time today? I'm working in an Internet café this morning, so you can also e-mail me.

Thanks very much,

Tamara

2 Look at the e-mail again and write when these things happen. Put them in the right order.

Tamara has problems.	*yesterday afternoon*	2
Her screen goes blank.	_____	
She gets a new computer.	_____	
Alex goes on holiday.	_____	
Tamara has an important meeting.	_____	
She works in an Internet café.	_____	

AN E-MAIL REPLY **3** 👥 Put these phrases in the right order and write Alex's reply.

Dear Tamara,	*1*
to hear from you.	
Regards, Alex	
but I'm in a meeting for the rest of the day.	
I'd really like to help	
Why don't you call a computer helpline?	
Thanks for your e-mail. It's good	

A COMPUTER HELPLINE **4** 🎧 Listen to the conversation between Tamara and the person on the computer helpline. Then answer these questions.

1 Which system does she have? Tick (✓) the right answer.
   Apple   Linux   Windows
2 What's on her screen?
3 What happens when she moves the mouse?
4 Does the man solve the problem?

5 🎧 👥 Here is a guide for people who work on the computer helpline. Write what they should say for points 1–4. Then listen to the phone conversation again and compare.

COMPUTER HELPLINE MANUAL

1   Start the conversation. _____

2   Ask for the person's name and phone number.
    _____

3   Ask about the person's system. _____

4   Ask about the problem. _____

NOW YOU **6** 👥 Role play this situation, using some of the language on these pages.

A Call a helpline about a problem with your computer. Turn to page 96.
B You work on a computer helpline. Turn to page 99.

Swap roles.

real world

Computers and the Internet

ARE YOU A COMPUTER PERSON?

1 Talk about your answers to these questions.

1 Which is more important to you?
   your computer   your TV
2 How do you usually contact your friends?
   by phone   by e-mail
3 Where do you usually look for information?
   in books   on the Internet

COMPUTER WORDS

2 Use these clues to help you complete the crossword opposite.

Across ▶

1 When there is a problem in your computer system, it can be because of a _____ . (5)
6 www is the world wide _____ . (3)
7 This man sent the first e-mail: _____ Tomlinson. (3)
8 The opposite of *on*. (3)
9 A short word for *network*. (3)
10 You use this to point and click. (5)
13 Another word for *information*. (4)
15 You look at this when you work on a computer. (6)
18 You can carry this kind of computer. (6)
19 When you have a problem with your computer, you phone a computer _____ . (8)

Down ▼

2 A machine that looks and acts like a person. (5)
3 When you move around the Internet from website to website, you _____ . (4)
4 When you type, you find the letters here. (8)
5 This company makes the Macintosh. (5)
6 Microsoft's famous operating system. (7)
11 You use this to connect your computer to the telephone line. (5)
12 The initials of *information technology*. (2)
14 @ means _____ . (2)
16 When your computer suddenly stops working, it's a _____ . (5)
17 The first page of a website is the _____ page. (4)

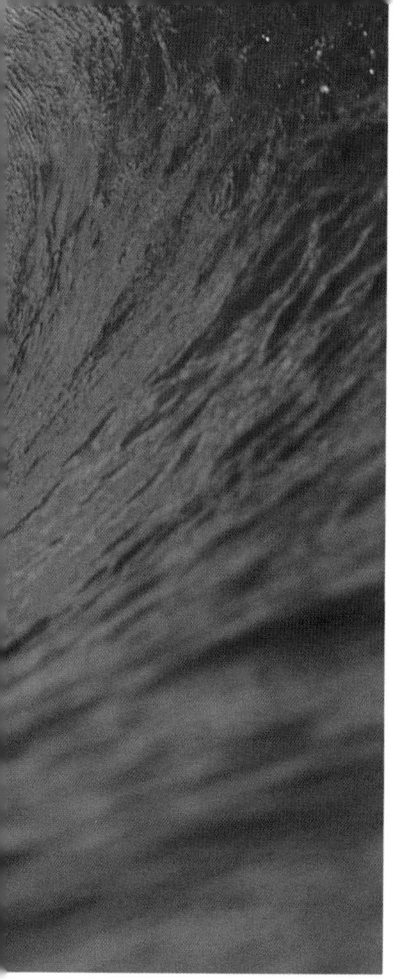

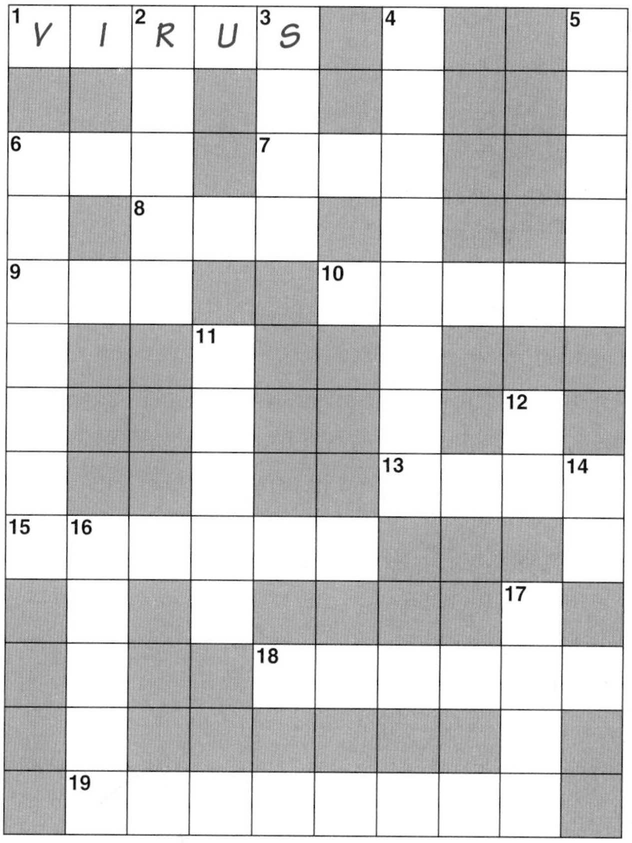

3 Some of the words in the crossword have other meanings in English. Can you match them to the photos on this page?

NOW YOU

4 Which words in the crossword can you put in these four groups?

- equipment
- the Internet
- problems
- systems

5 Can you add any words to the groups above?

8 careers

CAREER SUMMARIES

1 👥 Look at the summary of Anna Rezel's career opposite. Write these headings on the appropriate lines of the document.

> **Curriculum vitae**   **Qualifications**   **Profile**
> **Education**   **Interests**   **Work experience**

2 👥 Look at Tammy Vo's career summary opposite. Find words or phrases with similar meanings to the words in the table.

curriculum vitae	
specialist	
looking for	
job	
work experience	

EDUCATION

3 🎧 Listen to one of the women speaking about her education and the start of her career. Who is speaking – Anna or Tammy?

4 🎧 Fill the gaps with these words. Then listen to the first part again and check.

> **school**   **course**   **university**   **subjects**   **studied**   **research**

At _school_ I was very interested in math and physics. They were my favourite _____ . So, when I went to _____ , I _____ electrical engineering. At the end of the _____ I stayed at university for another year and did some _____ into systems management.

Curriculum vitae

Anna Rezel
via Spartaco 39, Milan, Italy
02 4536 1253
anrez11@casscass.net

A marketing specialist with experience in the advertising industry, Anna speaks excellent English and Italian. She is now looking for a job with an international media company in the UK.

| 2001 to present | Marketing manager, Cassanti & Cassanti advertising agency, Milan, Italy |
| 1999–2001 | Marketing assistant, Avanti & Driver advertising agency, London, UK |

| 1996–1999 | Leeds City University |
| 1991–1996 | Atherton Bridge School for Girls |

| BA (Hons) | Italian literature with business studies |
| A levels | Economics, History, Italian |

Going to the cinema, playing tennis and reading novels

RESUME

Tammy Vo

1376 Violet Parkway
Tucker Grove, CA 95646
(917) 0987-9876
tamvo06@sseal.com

An electrical engineer with experience of management, Tammy Vo is an expert in 3G systems for mobile telecommunications networks. She is now seeking a position as an engineer in a large telecom company in Malaysia or Singapore.

Employment history

2002 to present
  Staff Engineer, Oliphant Industries, Palo Alto, California
2001–2002
  Night manager, Cicadian Supermarket, Columbus, Ohio

Education

Bachelor of Science degree in Electrical Engineering, University of Ohio (2000)

GETTING A JOB

5 🎧 Put these events in the right order. Then listen to the second part again and check.

I had an interview.
I heard about a great opportunity.
I sent a resume and a letter.

I joined the company.
They offered me a job.
I left university.   *1*

NOW YOU

6 Use the language on these pages to write a short summary of your career.

7 👥 Show each other your career summaries and take turns to talk about your education and your first job.

I went to school in Shanghai.   *I joined my company in 2002.*

GRAMMAR Past simple (2)

PAST QUESTIONS   **1** 👥 Match the questions with the answers.

What did you do last night? ———————
When did you send your first e-mail?
Where were you on 31/12/99?
How many countries did you visit last year?
When were you born?
How did you come to this English class?

I was born on 16/6/71.
I was at a party with my family.
I think I sent it in 1997.
I came by taxi.
I visited two.
I worked at the office until
9:00 and then I went home.

2 👥 Take turns to ask the questions above and answer with your own information.

INTERVIEW QUESTIONS   **3** Use these phrases to make past simple questions.

> **leave your last job?**   **go to school?**
> **grow up?**   **be your first job?**
> **be born?**   **join your present company?**

Work experience
Why <u>*did you leave your last job*</u> ?
When _____ ?
What _____ ?

Personal history
Where _____ ?
Where _____ ?
Where _____ ?

4 🎧 Listen to part of a job interview. Put the questions above that the interviewer asks in the correct order.

CHECK Negatives and questions			
➕	➖	❓	**Short answers**
You worked.	You didn't work.	Did you work?	Yes, I did. / No, I didn't.
He went.	He didn't go.	Did he go?	Yes, he did. / No, he didn't.

❚ *Grammar reference page 105* ❚

NEGATIVES **5** 🎧 Listen to the interview again. Are these sentences true (T) or false (F)?

1 He wasn't born in New York.　　　　　　T
2 He didn't grow up in Manhattan.
3 He didn't go to Harvard.
4 He didn't get a job as a consultant.
5 He didn't join his present company in 2002.
6 He didn't like the long hours at McKinsey.

6 👥 Make questions from the sentences above. Take turns to ask and answer, using short answers.

> Was he born in New York?　　No, he wasn't.　　Did he grow up in Manhattan?　　No, he didn't.

7 Make these sentences negative.

1 I went to university.　　　　*I didn't go to university.*
2 He worked for the United Nations.　　_____
3 I was on holiday last week.　　_____
4 We lived in New Jersey.　　_____
5 She left the company.　　_____
6 They were in the office on Tuesday.　　_____

NOW YOU **8** 👥 Take turns to ask and answer questions about each other. Use the questions on these pages and make up others.

> Where were you born?　　I was born in Ankara.　　Did you grow up there?　　No, I didn't. I grew up in ...

PRONUNCIATION **A** 🎧 Listen and repeat. Notice the underlined vowel sounds.
/ɜː/ /eə/ /aʊ/ /ɪə/

/ɜː/	/eə/	/aʊ/	/ɪə/
work	where	how	appear
were	there	about	experience

B 🎧 Listen to these pairs of words. Do the underlined letters sound the same (✓) or different (✗)?

first – research　　　　here – thirty
dear – wear　　　　airport – idea
thousand – house　　　　now – word

working life   *Explanations*

DESCRIBING GRAPHS

1 🎧 Listen to a businesswoman describing the graph below to her boss. Answer these questions.

1 What does the graph show? Tick (✓) the right answer.
share prices   tax   sales figures   profit

2 Draw a line from these verbs to the part of the graph they describe.

go down
go up
stay the same

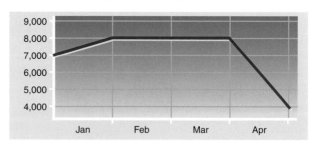

2 👥 Take turns. **A** Describe graph 1. **B** Describe graph 2.

Sales went down in …

1

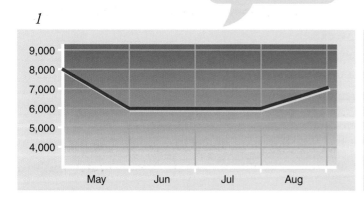

2

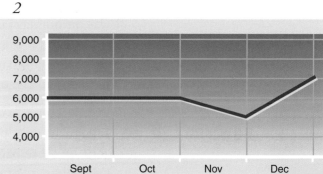

EXPLAINING A PROBLEM

3 🎧 Listen to the next part of the conversation between the woman and her boss. Tick (✓) the right answers to these questions.

1 What is Wiley's in London?
a big customer   a big warehouse

2 Why weren't there any products in the shops in April?
There was a problem in the office.
There was a problem at the factory.

3 Where was the boss at the time of the problem?
on holiday   in America

4 How does the boss sound during the conversation?
calm   angry

5 How does the woman sound?
nervous   confident

Why didn't you tell me about this?

NEGATIVE QUESTIONS

4 🎧 In the conversation, the boss asks a lot of negative questions. Write the negative questions, then listen again and check.

1 He didn't pay us. Why not? *Why didn't he pay us?*
2 There weren't any new products in the shops. Why not? _____
3 You weren't here. Why not? _____
4 You didn't tell me about this. Why not? _____
5 You didn't phone me. Why not? _____

> **CHECK** Negative past questions
>
> Why **didn't** you go there?
> Why **weren't** you there?
> Why **wasn't** he there?

NOW YOU

5 👥 Role play these situations, using some of the language on these pages.

▌**A** You asked B to contact you yesterday, but you didn't hear from him/her. Ask for an explanation. Use negative questions:

> *Why didn't you contact me yesterday?*

→ phone? → send an e-mail? → leave a message?

B Turn to page 99.

▌**B** A didn't go to a meeting with a customer yesterday. Ask negative questions:

> *Why didn't you go to the meeting yesterday?*

→ take the train? → get a taxi? → catch the bus?

A Turn to page 96.

▌**A** You are B's boss. You want to know why your sales figures went down last month. Listen to B's explanation and ask questions.
B Turn to page 99.

▌**B** You're A's boss. You want to know why your sales figures didn't go up last month. Listen to A's explanation and ask questions.
A Turn to page 96.

real world *A career story*

JOBS **1** Read the text below about the career of John Kao and <u>underline</u> his jobs. Which jobs are similar to these jobs?

musician   businessperson   writer   teacher   advisor

Some people have the same job for their whole life. But John Kao is a man who likes to move from one job to another. He's now famous as a consultant and entrepreneur. But he's also an author and a doctor. For fourteen years he was a university lecturer at Harvard and he was also once a teenage rock star!

KAO'S CAREER **2** The four texts at the top of the opposite page tell the story of the early years of John Kao. Read them and put them in the right order.

3 Look at the verbs in green in the four texts. They are all irregular verbs in the past simple. Use them to complete this table.

come	*came*	do		get	
grow		hear		know	
learn		meet		read	
say		see		take	
teach		win		write	

4 Listen to part two of the story of John Kao's career. Then fill the gaps in the text opposite with the past simple of some of the verbs above.

NOW YOU **5** Write some sentences about your career, using some of the language on these pages. Then compare with your partner.

I grew up in Cairo.
I studied business at university.

JOHN KAO PART ONE

☐ John Kao's parents were from China, but he grew up in New York City in the 1950s and 1960s. For John, it was a very interesting experience. He once said, 'At school I was in an American world, but I came home to a Chinese world. I was like a cultural astronaut.' Kao did well at school, and at home he learnt the piano.

☐ First, Kao studied philosophy at Yale University; then, he trained as a doctor at Harvard Medical School. But that wasn't enough. After that, he took a business course at the Harvard Business School. Kao soon knew that business was the subject for him. When he finished his course, he got a job as a university lecturer in business.

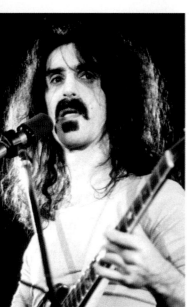

☐ In 1969, when he was eighteen, Kao wrote to the rock star, Frank Zappa, and asked to join his band. Zappa listened to Kao's music and liked what he heard. So Kao moved to Los Angeles and played keyboards for Zappa's band, The Mothers of Invention. It was a fantastic experience, but Kao really wanted to go to university.

☐ For the next fourteen years, Kao taught business at Harvard. But he was always interested in new ideas. One day, he met Steven Soderbergh, a young film director. Soderbergh talked about his new film and said that he needed money. Kao read Soderbergh's script and saw a business opportunity. So he worked as Soderbergh's producer. Together, they got the money and the film was a very big success; in fact, it won the top prize at the Cannes Film Festival in 1989.

JOHN KAO PART TWO

In 1986, Kao _heard_ about some interesting research at the Harvard Medical School. A professor showed him how he _____ sheets of human skin in his laboratory. Because Kao was a doctor and also _____ about business, he _____ an opportunity. He _____ the professor's idea and started a small bio-tech company.

'I _____ everything,' _____ Kao. 'I _____ the business plan, I _____ the money and I employed the managers.'

Before long, Kao's small company was worth millions of dollars.

Over the next few years, Kao started more small companies. He also _____ a successful book about his ideas, called _Jamming_. When other businesspeople _____ his book, they _____ to him and asked for his advice. By 1996 Kao was so busy that he stopped teaching at the Harvard Business School and started a company called Idea Factory.

Today, Idea Factory is a way for Kao to share his ideas and his advice with other businesspeople. It's also a way for him to make a very good profit!

review 4

VOCABULARY
Regular and irregular verbs

1 In the past tense, which of these verbs are regular and which are irregular? Put them in the correct group.

need	leave	appear	go	show
work	write	start	get	hear

regular   irregular

2 Write the past form of the irregular verbs above.

_____ _____ _____ _____ _____

3 Look back at Units 7 and 8 and add at least five verbs to each of the groups above.

GRAMMAR CHECK

4 Make these sentences negative.

1 He liked the music.   *He didn't like the music.*
2 We stayed at the Grand Hotel. _____
3 They were in Germany last month. _____
4 She talked about the new film. _____
5 I took the train.   _____
6 He was at the meeting.   _____

5 Put these words in the right order to make questions in the past simple.

1 you / did / meet / where   *Where did you meet?*
2 do / he / did / what / yesterday _____
3 last week / go / did / where / they _____
4 last night / you / were / where _____
5 here / come / did / how / you   _____
6 you / have / a holiday / did / last year _____
7 what / finish / time / you / did / report / the _____
8 at / restaurant / at / she / o'clock / was / eight / the _____

FOCUS ON ...
Giving reasons

6 We often use the infinitive (*to* + verb) to give reasons for actions.

> They stayed late at the office.

> Why?

> To finish the report.

7 Match the two parts of these sentences.

1 They go to Paris every year — to invite him for an interview.
2 He travelled all night — to get some information.
3 They sent him an e-mail — to study engineering.
4 She's surfing the Internet — to discuss the plans.
5 They had a meeting — to be at the breakfast meeting.
6 She went to university — to visit the Louvre.

PRONUNCIATION
/d/ /t/ /ɪd/

A Listen and repeat. Notice the underlined sounds.

/d/	/t/
do	two
day	today
doctor	teacher

B Listen and repeat the past forms of these verbs. Notice the difference in the sound of the final -ed.

/d/	/t/	/ɪd/
showed	asked	started

C Listen to the endings of these -ed verbs. Which of the verbs above do they sound like? Write them in the correct column.

watched   appeared   interrupted   realised   laughed
finished   played   visited   listened

seventy-five **75**

9 on the **move**

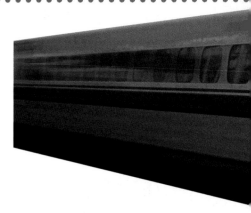

TRAVEL WORDS   **1**   Complete the vocabulary network with these words.

> boarding gate   accidents   suitcase   ticket office
> passport   check-in   visa   driving licence   cancellations
> platform   hand luggage   delays   traffic jams

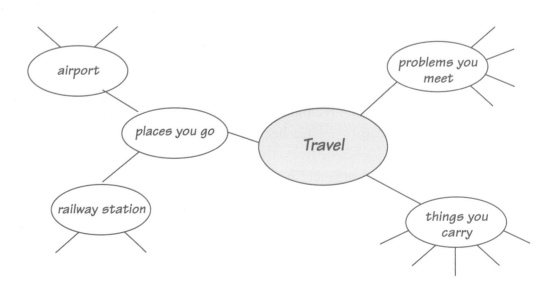

2   Add other words that you know to the network.

PRONUNCIATION   **A**   Listen and repeat. Notice the <u>underlined</u> sounds.
/f/ /v/ /w/

/f/	/v/	/w/
<u>f</u>light	<u>v</u>isa	<u>w</u>here
tra<u>ff</u>ic	dri<u>v</u>ing	net<u>w</u>ork

B   Listen and repeat these phrases. Concentrate on the /f/, /v/ and /w/ sounds.

foreign office   platform fifty-five   travel advisor   working women
the world's worst visitor

CHECKING IN   **3** 🎧   Fill the gaps with the singular or plural of some of the words in the network opposite. Then listen and check.

> ■ Good morning. Can I check in for Kuala Lumpur, please?
>
> ○ Of course. Can I see your ticket and your _____ , please? Thank you. Are you checking in any luggage?
>
> ■ Yes. These two _____ .
>
> ○ OK. And do you have any _____ ?
>
> ■ Just this.
>
> ○ Good. Now, I'm afraid there's a short _____ on the flight this morning. So, can you go to _____ 32 at 11:55? Here's your boarding pass.
>
> ■ Thank you.
>
> ○ Have a good flight.

LATE FOR WORK   **4** 🎧   Listen to a man explaining why he is late for work and answer these questions.

1 What's his excuse today? _____
2 What was his excuse yesterday? _____
3 What was his excuse the day before that? _____

NOW YOU   **5** 👥   Talk about these questions.

1 When did you last make a long journey?
2 Was it a holiday, a business trip or a visit to family or friends?
3 How did you travel?
4 What did you take with you?
5 Did you have any problems?

GRAMMAR *can* and *have to*

TRAVEL INFORMATION

1 👥 Look at these pairs of sentences and tick (✓) the ones which describe the signs above them.

You can go in the water.
You can't go in the water.

You can't give food to the birds.
You have to give food to the birds.

You can be careful.
You have to be careful.

You have to stand on the right.
You don't have to stand on the right.

LEAVING KATHERINE

2 🎧 Two tourists are trying to get from the small town of Katherine to Darwin in north Australia. Listen to the conversation at the information centre and answer these questions.

1 When do they have to be in Darwin? _____

2 Why can't they take a train? _____

3 Do they have to hire a car? _____

4 Can they hire a car today? _____

5 Do they have to have an international driving licence? _____

CHECK *can* and *have to*

Possible/allowed	*You can*
Not possible/allowed	*You can't*
Necessary	*You have to*
Not necessary	*You don't have to*

■ *Grammar reference pages 102 and 104* ■

SINGAPORE REPORT

3 Listen to a report for travellers to Singapore. Then use these prompts to write sentences with *can/can't* or *have to / don't have to.*

1 get a visa   *You don't have to get a visa.*
2 worry about health problems   _____
3 pay to use some roads   _____
4 buy a licence to drive in the
    downtown area   _____
5 drive on the left   _____
6 smoke in most public places   _____
7 take chewing gum into the country _____

**ASKING FOR
INFORMATION**

4 **A** You are planning a trip to Moscow.
Use these prompts to ask B for information.
B Turn to page 99 and answer A's questions.

get a visa?
take warm clothes?
take a train from the airport to the city centre?
hire a car?

> Can I … ?   Do I have to … ?

5 **B** You are planning a trip to Johannesburg. Use these prompts to ask A for information. **A** Turn to page 96 and answer B's questions.

drink the water?   book a taxi from the airport?
use my mobile phone?   take cash out of the country?

6 Use the language on these pages to talk about other countries that you know.

> In the UK you have
> to drive on the left.   In the USA you can't smoke
> in most public places.

working life *Managing e-mail*

E-MAIL AND YOU

1 Talk about your answers to these questions.

1 How many e-mails do you normally get a day?
2 What percentage (%) do you delete immediately?
3 What percentage do you read immediately?
4 What percentage do you reply to?

CHECKING AN INBOX

2 Owais Khan arrives at work one morning and finds the e-mails opposite in his inbox. Read them quickly and answer these questions.

1 Which e-mail does he have to answer now? _____
2 Which e-mails doesn't he have to answer? _____
3 Which e-mails ask for advice? _____
4 Which phrases ask for advice? Complete these questions.
Do you have _____ ?
What can you _____ ?

AN E-MAIL REPLY

3 Read the reply to one of the e-mails and answer these questions.

1 Which e-mail does it answer? _____
2 What two pieces of advice does he give? _____

_____

3 Which phrases does he use to give his advice? Fill the gaps.
Why _____ _____ ... ?   How _____ ... ?

Thanks for your e-mail. I'm afraid I don't know much about business in
India. Why don't you search for 'business in India' on the Internet?
Or, how about asking in your local bookshop? There are a lot of good
books on business in different countries.
I'm sorry I can't be more helpful!
Owais

NOW YOU

4 Write a reply to the marketing department at Owais's company. Thank them for their e-mail and give them some advice. Then compare your e-mails.

5 Write e-mails to each other, asking for advice about where to go on holiday next year. Then swap e-mails and write replies, giving each other some advice.

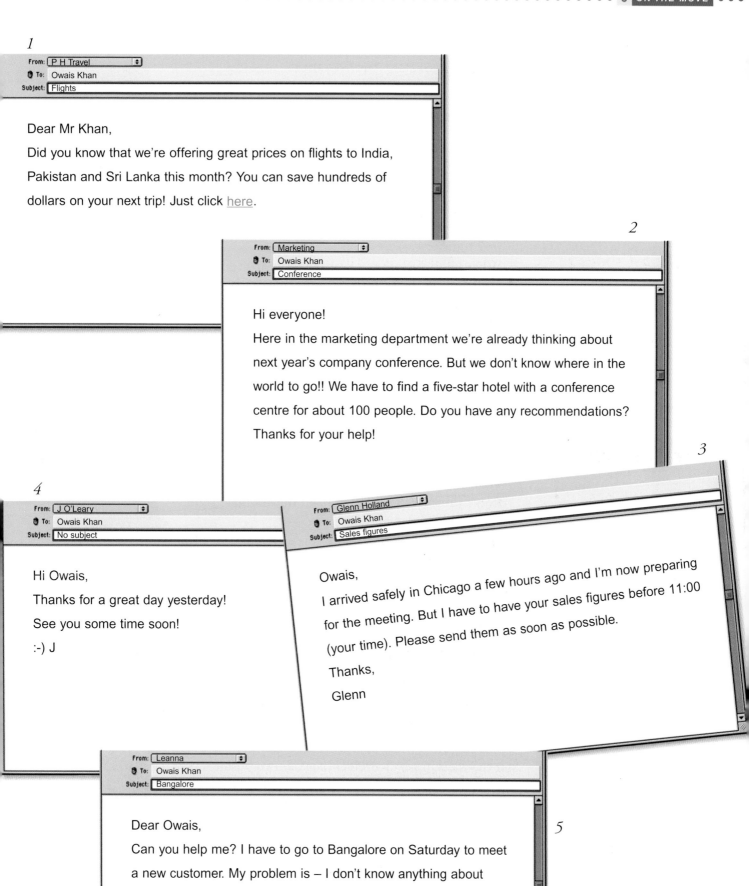

1

From: P H Travel
To: Owais Khan
Subject: Flights

Dear Mr Khan,

Did you know that we're offering great prices on flights to India, Pakistan and Sri Lanka this month? You can save hundreds of dollars on your next trip! Just click here.

2

From: Marketing
To: Owais Khan
Subject: Conference

Hi everyone!

Here in the marketing department we're already thinking about next year's company conference. But we don't know where in the world to go!! We have to find a five-star hotel with a conference centre for about 100 people. Do you have any recommendations? Thanks for your help!

3

From: Glenn Holland
To: Owais Khan
Subject: Sales figures

Owais,

I arrived safely in Chicago a few hours ago and I'm now preparing for the meeting. But I have to have your sales figures before 11:00 (your time). Please send them as soon as possible.

Thanks,

Glenn

4

From: J O'Leary
To: Owais Khan
Subject: No subject

Hi Owais,

Thanks for a great day yesterday!

See you some time soon!

:-) J

5

From: Leanna
To: Owais Khan
Subject: Bangalore

Dear Owais,

Can you help me? I have to go to Bangalore on Saturday to meet a new customer. My problem is – I don't know anything about India! Help! Where can I find some information about the country? What can you suggest?

Many thanks,

Leanna

real world

Different cultures

TRAVEL WORRIES

1  When people travel, which of these questions do they worry about?

1 How do I say 'Hello' when I meet people for the first time?

2 What kind of clothes do I have to wear?

3 Do I have to arrive early for meetings?

4 What kind of tips do I give to people like waiters and taxi drivers?

TIPPING

2 Read and listen to this story. Then answer these questions.

1 In the story, what's the normal tip for a waiter?

2 Why do you think the businessmen left such a big tip?

3 Which country do you think this story comes from? (Turn to page 101 to find out if you're right.)

The world's biggest tip

In this city, you always have to leave a tip. When you take a cab, you usually give the driver a 10 per cent tip. When you have a haircut, you leave the hairdresser 15 per cent. And when you eat in a restaurant, the waiter usually gets a 20 per cent tip. Usually – but not always. In April 2001, two businessmen walked into one of the city's busiest restaurants after a very good day's work. They said to the waiter, 'We'd like to buy a drink for everyone here.' Then they ordered a very, very expensive meal. When they asked for the check, the waiter was worried: it was for around $9,000.

But the check wasn't a problem for the two businessmen. They were happy to pay and they even added a tip of $15,000 for the waiter!

GLOSSARY

check (US) = *bill* (UK)

3 Now talk about these questions.

1 What kind of tips do you give in your country to …
a taxi driver?   a hairdresser?
a waiter in a restaurant?   a waiter in a bar?

2 What kinds of tips do you give in other countries that you know?

BUSINESS CARDS

4 🎧 👥 Read and listen to this story. Then answer these questions.

1 In the story, how do people usually offer their business cards?
2 What do they usually do when they receive a business card?
3 What does the man do wrong?
4 Which country do you think this story comes from? (Turn to page 101 to find out if you're right.)

A bad introduction

It was the boss's first day in his new job, so he walked around the office and introduced himself to everyone. He offered his business card to each person in the usual way: he held it with two hands, so that the other person could read it easily.

'I don't want your business card. I already know who you are.'

But one man in the office said, 'I don't want your business card. I already know who you are.'

'Please take it,' said the boss and smiled.

Slowly, the man took the business card … and then he folded it in two.

Everyone in the office knew that this was very rude. When you receive a business card in this country, you always have to read it very carefully.

In fact, the next day the story was in the newspapers and the boss got more than 10,000 e-mails of support from people right across the country.

He folded the business card in two.

5 👥 Now talk about these questions.

1 How do people give and receive business cards in your country?
2 What do people do with business cards in other countries that you know?

NOW YOU **6** 👥 In what other ways is working life different in your country from other countries that you know? Talk about these questions.

1 What kind of clothes do people wear to a business meeting?
2 When you have a meeting, what time do you arrive? A few minutes early? Exactly on time? A few minutes late?
3 Do businesspeople give gifts to colleagues or customers? When? What sort of gifts do they give?

10 in the **news**

TOP STORIES

1 👥 Quickly look at the headlines opposite. Which of these subjects do you think the stories are about?

politics

business

entertainment

sport

2 👥 Put three of these words in each of the groups above.

pop   match   reforms   stock market

hits   stadium   parliament   currency

injury   band   share prices   government

3 Read the texts of the articles and fill the gaps with the words above.

4 👥 Read the texts again and answer these questions.

1 What kind of week was it on Wall Street?
2 Who is leaving the Spice Girls?
3 How popular is Mr Koizumi?
4 Who is going to play in tonight's big football match?
5 Where is there going to be confusion?
6 What do these initials stand for?
    EU   PM   US

NOW YOU

5 👥👥 Write a headline and one or two sentences about a story in the news.

US SHARES CRASH

Yesterday Wall Street had its worst day for over ten years at the end of a terrible week for the _____ . The biggest falls were in the _____ of companies in the high-tech and Internet sectors.

Spice Girls say 'STOP!'

It looks like the world's top girl _____ is saying 'Stop right now, thank you very much.' After years at the top of the music business, Sporty Spice (Melanie C) said yesterday that she is leaving the _____ group. The girls had a number of huge international _____ in the late 1990s.

Ronaldo out again

There's more bad news for Brazilian soccer fans. Doctors say that Ronaldo, the world's most famous footballer, has another _____ problem and is not going to play for Brazil in this evening's big _____ against Chile at Couto Pereira _____ in Curitiba. Brazilians are now asking, 'Is he going to be ready for the World Cup?'

Koizumi becomes new PM

Junichori Koizumi became Japan's new Prime Minister after a vote in _____ yesterday afternoon. At the moment, the 59-year-old Koizumi is very popular in the country, but he says he's going to introduce some tough _____ .

A Happy New Euro

Europeans are waking up this morning to a new year and a new _____ . Eleven countries in the European Union (EU) are introducing the new Euro notes and coins today. A spokeswoman for the French _____ said, 'There's going to be some confusion in Europe over the next few days, but we don't expect any serious problems.'

GRAMMAR The *going to* future

WEATHER AND TRAVEL

1 🎧 Listen to part of a local radio programme and tick (✓) the correct answers to these questions.

1 What's the weather going to be like in San Berdino today?
  hot and sunny   cold and wet

2 What's going to happen at the city airport?
  There are going to be cancellations.   There are going to be delays.

3 Are there going to be a lot of problems on the roads?
  Yes, there are.   No, there aren't.

2 🎧 Listen again and fill the gaps with these phrases.

it's going to be	**you're going to feel**	**We're going to see**
there's going to be	**There aren't going to be**	**there are going to be**

Now the weather. Well, *it's going to be*   a lovely day in San Berdino today. _____ a lot of sunshine, and if you're out this afternoon, _____ the heat! Forty-two degrees is today's top temperature! Travel news. After yesterday's problems at San Berdino Airport, the situation is returning to normal this morning. _____ any more cancellations, although I'm afraid _____ some delays on international flights. On the roads, no problems! But don't forget the big match at the City Stadium this evening. It's the S B Bluesocks against D C Thumpers, so _____ a lot of traffic around the stadium just before 7:00.

CHECK The *going to* future

➕	➖	❓	Short answers
You're going to be …	You aren't going to be …	Are you going to be … ?	Yes. I am. / No, I'm not.
He's going to be …	He isn't going to be …	Is he going to be … ?	Yes, he is. / No, he isn't.

❙ *Grammar reference page 103* ❙

NEWS HEADLINES **3** Look at the newspaper headlines. Are the sentences below true (T) or false (F)? Rewrite the false ones.

No new airport for Montreal

Prince William cancels trip to Australia

Beijing gets next Olympics

American economy to get worse next year

Marat to miss Wimbledon after injury

Experts say stock market to fall again

1 The next Olympic Games are going to be in Beijing.
2 There's going to be a new airport in Montreal.
3 Share prices are going to go up.
4 Prince William isn't going to visit Australia.
5 Safin Marat is going to play at Wimbledon.
6 The American economy is going to get better next year.

4 Write sentences about these headlines, using the *going to* future.

Thai government to introduce reforms next year

Bush cancels visit to Japan

Tyson to fight again next year

Computer company to close three factories

Schroder and Jospin to meet in Berlin

No agreement this year on tax changes

FUTURE QUESTIONS **5** Use these prompts to write questions with the *going to* future.

1 It's your decision, so … what / you / do? *what are you going to do?*
2 They aren't going to meet tomorrow, so … when / they / meet?
3 We don't have any currency, so … how / we / pay?
4 Her train is cancelled, so … how / she / get home?
5 The restaurant is closed, so … where / we / eat?
6 The hotels are all full, so … where / they / stay?

NOW YOU **6** Use the *going to* future to talk about the weather and travel today or tomorrow in your area.

I think it's going to be hot this afternoon.

There are going to be problems on the roads tomorrow morning.

working life *Opinions*

COMPANY WORDS

1 Match these phrases to their descriptions.

an announcement	when a company introduces a new product
job cuts	when managers tell people important news
a takeover	when people lose their jobs
a product launch	when a company buys another company

2 Listen to a conversation between three employees of a big company. Tick (✓) the three phrases above that you hear.

OPINIONS

3 Listen to the conversation again. Number these speech bubbles in the order that you hear them.

> *I'm sure it's going to be good news. I reckon it's going to be a product launch or something like that.*

> *In my opinion, nothing's going to change. We have these announcements every six months. They're always the same.*

> *I think it's going to be bad news. My guess is there are going to be some more job cuts.*

4 Look at the speech bubbles again. How many phrases can you find that introduce an opinion? Add to the list.

introducing an opinion

In my opinion

AGREEING AND DISAGREEING

5 Look at these phrases. Which are for agreeing and which are for disagreeing? Write *A* or *D* next to them.

I'm afraid I have to disagree.   That's right.
I completely agree.   That's nonsense.
I'm sorry, but I don't agree.   That's a good point.

6 Listen to the conversation again. Tick (✓) the phrases above that you hear. Which one of them is not very polite?

WHAT DO YOU THINK?

7 Look at these covers of the international magazine, *The Economist*. What do you think the main story inside the magazine is about? (Use the words in the box to help you.)

Give your opinions and agree or disagree. (Turn to page 101 to see if you are right.)

I think it's about the Internet.

Yes, I agree.

the Internet   politics   sport
the stock market   new products
currencies   the weather   war

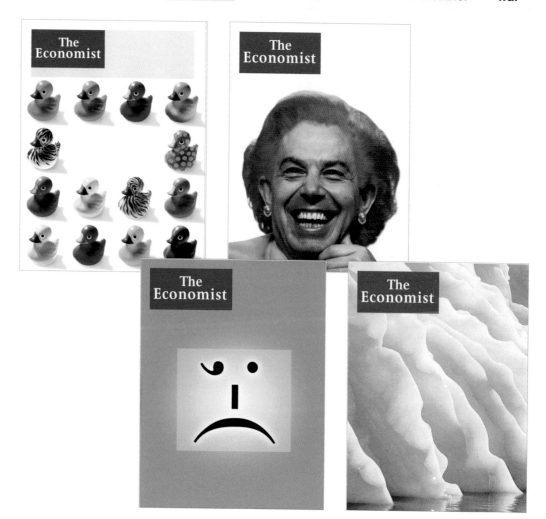

NOW YOU

8 Talk about these things that are/aren't going to happen in your company or in the news. Give your opinions and agree/disagree about what's going to happen next.

job cuts   a sporting event   a takeover   a film/pop star

I think Real Madrid are going to win on Sunday.

I don't agree. Barcelona are going to win!

real world

Your future career?

SUCCESS AND FAILURE

1 In a person's career, which of these words are positive and which are negative? Put them in the correct group.

unemployment   rejection   a pay rise
a pay cut   a promotion   the sack
a bonus   opportunity

positive

negative

THE GAME

2 In this game, your objective is to be the boss. To play, toss a coin. Heads: go forward one square. Tails: go forward two squares. When you land on a square, do what it says. If you don't know what to say, go back three squares.

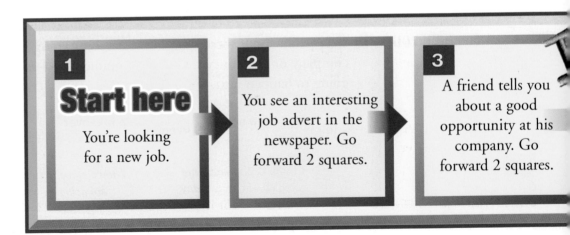

1 Start here
You're looking for a new job.

2 You see an interesting job advert in the newspaper. Go forward 2 squares.

3 A friend tells you about a good opportunity at his company. Go forward 2 squares.

16 Your company is going to launch a new product. Stand up and make the announcement.

17 Your boss gets another job. Say something nice to him/her before he/she goes.

18 **Congratulations!** You're the boss.

15 Your sales were down by 30% last month. Say why.

14 You interview someone for a job. Ask three questions about the person's work experience.

13 An American customer is visiting you for the first time. Tell him three things about business life in your country.

10 You meet the boss of the company for the first time. Think of three questions to start the conversation.

11 You get a promotion! Go up the ladder.

12 Your manager's computer crashes. Give him/her two pieces of advice.

9 You get the sack. Go down the ladder

8 You had travel problems and you were an hour late for work this morning. Say why.

7 You take a call for your manager, but he/she doesn't want to speak to the caller. What do you say?

4 A job interview. Say three things about your career.

5 A job interview. Say why you left your last job.

6 It's your first day in your new job. Introduce yourself and say three things about yourself.

review 5

**VOCABULARY
Crossword**

1 Complete this crossword with words from Units 9 and 10.

Across ▶

1 When a flight isn't going to happen it's a _____ . (12)

5 The currency of Europe. (4)

6 You play important football matches here. (7)

9 He didn't have any money _____ he didn't pay. (2)

10 The opposite of *yes*. (2)

12 The stock _____ . (6)

13 You can't take chewing _____ into Singapore. (3)

14 Don't swim near one of these! (9)

18 You find this in Hollywood and in the night sky. (4)

19 You have to have a _____ pass to get on a plane. (8)

20 The week after this week is _____ week. (4)

22 You sometimes have to have this to enter a country. (4)

23 The opposite of *small*. (3)

24 You have to buy this before you travel on a plane, train or bus. (6)

25 When you have the same opinion, you _____ . (5)

Down ▼

1 _____ gum. (7)

2 You're doing a _____word. (5)

3 You climb this in your career. (6)

4 Something that doesn't make sense is _____ . (8)

7 The day after today. (8)

8 The past of *meet*. (3)

11 The opposite of *inside*. (7)

14 Another word for *taxi*. (3)

15 When you meet people you give them a business _____ . (4)

16 You have to have a _____ licence for a car. (7)

17 When you get on a plane you can carry hand _____ . (7)

20 The short form of *Internet*. (3)

21 A successful pop song. (3)

23 The infinitive form of *I am, you are*. (2)

GRAMMAR CHECK

2 Complete the sentences, using *can/can't* or *have to / don't have to*.

> **Admission**
> Adults $5
> Children under 16 Free

1 You _____ pay for children.

2 You _____ use cameras.

Smoking area

3 You _____ smoke.

4 You _____ wear a seat belt.

3 Write sentences about the future. Put the <u>underlined</u> verbs into the positive or negative with *going to*.

1 The next Olympic Games / <u>be</u> in Beijing.   _____

2 More and more people / <u>speak</u> English.   _____

3 Before I die / I <u>make</u> a million dollars.   _____

4 An American rocket / <u>land</u> on Jupiter next year.   _____

5 Elvis Presley / <u>have</u> another hit song.   _____

FOCUS ON ...
Past, present and future

4 Put the verbs in brackets ( ) into the correct tense.

1 I (not see) _____ him last week, but I (have) _____ lunch with him yesterday.

2 She's a really good manager. She (not have)_____ a secretary, so she (make) _____ all her arrangements herself.

3 He (not listen)_____ to you at the moment, because he (watch) _____ TV.

4 They (not take)_____ the car on holiday next month, because they (fly) _____ .

PRONUNCIATION
/θ/ /ð/

A 🎧 Listen and repeat. Notice the difference between the 'th' sounds.

/θ/	/ð/
<u>th</u>ree	<u>th</u>ere
ba<u>th</u>	clo<u>th</u>es

B 🎧 Listen to the <u>underlined</u> sounds. Put the words into one of the two groups above.

<u>th</u>ank you   <u>th</u>an   ano<u>th</u>er   no<u>th</u>ing   <u>th</u>irty
<u>th</u>ey   <u>th</u>e   <u>th</u>ink

interactions

Student A

ASKING QUESTIONS   Unit 2 *page 17*   exercise **5**

Tina Magnusson

Services Director

Santis Direct

Napapiiri   tina.magnuss@santis.com
32467 Rovaniemi   00 767 878 00 (W)
Finland   00 767 786 99 (H)

NOW YOU   Unit 3 *page 27*   exercise **7**

▪ In this diary, write two things that you always do, two things that you never do and two things that you sometimes do. Then get ready for B's call.

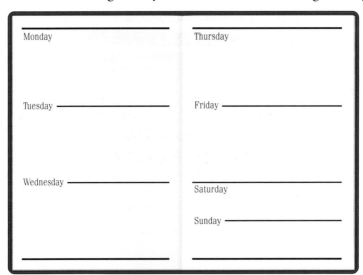

Monday

Tuesday —————————

Wednesday ——————————

Thursday

Friday ————————

Saturday

Sunday ———————

▪ Call B. You want to have a meeting with him/her before Wednesday afternoon. You can meet at these times.

    1   a breakfast meeting in the company canteen at 7:30 on Monday morning
    2   a meeting in your office at 6:30 on Tuesday evening
    3   lunch at 1:15 on Wednesday

NOW YOU   Unit 4 *page 35* exercise **4**

Give B directions from the country club to the Girl from Ipanema bar.

NOW YOU   Unit 6 *page 51* exercise **6**

The man on the right usually drives Formula One racing cars. In the picture, he's wearing a bow tie and riding a monocycle because he's raising money for charity. He lives in Monaco and his name's Mika Hakkinen.

NOW YOU   Unit 6 *page 53* exercise **7**

▌ Customer information:
You're looking for a sports bag and some running shoes. You don't want to pay more than $30 for the bag.

▌ Shop assistant information:
The cheapest tennis racquet in your shop costs $30, but you can sell it for $28.50, if the customer pays cash.

NOW YOU   Unit 7 *page 59* exercise **6**

Ask questions:
1 When / first passenger railway journey?
2 When / the first TV broadcast?

The answers to B's questions are:
1 The first radio advert was on 28/8/1922. It was an advert for the Queensboro Corporation in New York.
2 The Queen of England's first e-mail was on 26/3/1976. She was probably on the Internet before Bill Gates!

NOW YOU   Unit 7 *page 61* exercise **5**

Use these prompts to tell the story of the first TV advert:
1/7/41 New Yorkers watch TV
TV station interrupts programme
Bulova watch appears
stays for 60 seconds
the first TV advert!

NOW YOU   Unit 7 *page 63*   exercise **6**

▌ Your computer problem:
You have an Apple computer. A few minutes ago some numbers appeared on your screen and the computer went 'bleep-bleep-bleep'. Phone B to ask for help. Answer the questions that he or she asks you.

▌ Your helpline solution:
When B calls you, do the following:
1   Start the conversation.
2   Ask for B's name and phone number.
3   Ask about B's system.
4   Ask about the problem.
5   Ask if the keyboard works.
6   Tell B to switch off the computer and switch it on again.
7   If that doesn't work, ask if you can call back later.

NOW YOU   Unit 8 *page 71*   exercise **5**

▌ Apologise to B and explain that there was a problem with your car yesterday. You also live a long way from the railway station in a place where there aren't any buses. You called for a taxi, but it didn't come.

▌ Reasons that sales stayed the same:
There wasn't any advertising for your product on TV.
A lot of your customers were on holiday.
There were new taxes on your products.

NOW YOU   Unit 9 *page 79*   exercise **5**

Johannesburg – information for visitors:
Johannesburg is South Africa's number one business city and life is easy here for business travellers. You can drink the water and you can use your mobile phone with no problems. You have to book a taxi to go from the airport to the city centre when you arrive. And, when you leave, remember that you can't take a lot of cash out of the country.

Student B

ASKING QUESTIONS   Unit 2 *page 17*   exercise **5**

TUGGERANONG **SYSTEMS**

Tuggeranong Systems
Stromlo Buildings 1212
Canberra
Australia

Michael Woo
Information Systems
Manager

mike.woo02@tugger.au
00 878 654 89 (W)
00 856 878 88 (H)

NOW YOU   Unit 3 *page 27*   exercise **7**

▌ Call A. You want to arrange a meeting, but you are only in A's city at the weekend. You can meet at these times.

1 a meeting in A's office on Sunday afternoon at 4:30
2 dinner in a restaurant at 7:45 on Saturday evening
3 a breakfast meeting in your hotel at 7:15 on Monday

▌ In this diary, write two things that you always do, two things that you never do and two things that you sometimes do. Then get ready for A's call.

Monday	Thursday
Tuesday ——————	Friday ——————
Wednesday ——————	Saturday ——————
	Sunday ——————

NOW YOU Unit 4 *page 35* exercise **4**

Give A directions from the gym on the beach to Peace Square.

NOW YOU Unit 6 *page 51* exercise **6**

The man on the left is wearing a T-shirt and jeans because he's playing the guitar with his band, The Rock Bottom Remainders. But this man is a writer, not a musician. At his home in Maine in the USA, he writes some of the world's most popular horror stories. His most famous books include *Carrie, The Shining* and *Misery*. His name's Stephen King.

NOW YOU Unit 6 *page 53* exercise **7**

▌ Shop assistant information:
You work in a shop. You sell two different kinds of sports bag. The cheaper bag is $20; the more expensive bag is normally $35. You don't sell running shoes, but the shop round the corner sells them.

▌ Customer information:
You're looking for a new tennis racquet and you want to buy the cheapest one in the shop. You want to pay by credit card and you want a receipt.

NOW YOU Unit 7 *page 59* exercise **6**

Ask questions:
1 When / first radio advert?
2 When / Queen of England's first e-mail?

The answers to A's questions are:
1 The first passenger railway journey was between Stockton and Darlington in the UK in 1825.
2 The first TV broadcast was on 14/6/1923 in the USA.

NOW YOU Unit 7 *page 61* exercise **5**

Use these prompts to tell the story of the first phone call:
first phone call 10/3/75
Alexander Graham Bell calls his assistant
'Mr Watson, come here, I want you.'
businessmen laugh at the idea
Bell starts his own company – American Telephone and Telegraph

NOW YOU   Unit 7 *page 63* exercise **6**

▌ Your helpline solution:
When A calls you, do the following:
1 Start the conversation.
2 Ask for A's name and phone number.
3 Ask about A's system.
4 Ask about the problem.
5 Say that you can't help at the moment. Ask if you can call back later.

▌ Your computer problem:
You use a Linux system. Your screen and your keyboard are fine, but nothing happens when you move the mouse. Phone A to ask for help. Answer the questions that he or she asks you.

NOW YOU   Unit 8 *page 71* exercise **5**

▌ Apologise to A and explain that you were out of the office all day yesterday and you didn't have your laptop computer with you. You tried to use your mobile phone but it didn't work.

▌ Reasons that sales went down:
There was a big problem at your warehouse.
Your competitors did a lot of advertising.
You were on holiday for two weeks.

NOW YOU   Unit 9 *page 79* exercise **4**

Moscow – information for visitors:
Before you visit Moscow, remember that you have to get a visa to enter the country. You also have to take some warm clothes, because the city can be very cold! There aren't any trains from Moscow's main airport to the city centre, so when you arrive, take a taxi to your hotel. (You can hire cars at the airport, but there are often bad traffic jams in the city centre, so this is not a very good idea.)

NOW YOU   Unit 2 *page 19*   exercise **5**

INFORMATION FOR NEW EMPLOYEES

What's this?

- cheese
- avocado
- mushroom
- egg
- cucumber
- tomato
- smoked salmon
- prawn
- tuna
- chicken

How much is it?

FOOD

A sandwich with one filling is $3.50.
Example: A cheese sandwich is $3.50.

A sandwich with two fillings is $4.00.
Example: A cheese and prawn sandwich is $4.00.

A sandwich with three fillings is $4.25.
Example: A cheese, prawn and mushroom sandwich is $4.25.

Always ask the customer:

Just … ?
How about some … ?

DRINK

Orange juice	$1.25
Cola	$1.00
Milk	$0.75
Coffee	$1.00

CHECK Prices

$1.25 = one dollar twenty-five
$0.75 = seventy-five cents

Facts

COMPARING PLACES

Unit 4 *page 32* exercise **1**

1 According to *The Economist* magazine, life is around 50 per cent cheaper in New York than in Tokyo.
2 Los Angeles has the most expensive taxis in the world. It costs around $15 for a 5km trip.
3 Johannesburg is more dangerous than Rome. According to some travel writers, it is the most dangerous city in the world.
4 The safest drivers in the world are in Sweden. There are only 1.8 deaths per 10,000 vehicles every year.
5 London has worse pollution than Reykjavik. (People in Iceland say that Reykjavik is the cleanest city in the world – but it is a lot smaller than London!)
6 Bangkok. 82% of journeys in the city are by car, motorbike or taxi, and the average speed in the centre is often less than 10kph.
7 Luxembourg. According to *The Economist*, this small country has the best standard of living in Europe.
8 Rio de Janerio, of course! (The other two cities are a long way from the sea.)

DATES

Unit 7 *page 59* exercise **3**

The first phone call was on 10 March 1875.
The first passenger flight was on 1 January 1914.
The first TV advert was on 1 July 1941.
The first e-mail was in 1971.
The first tourist flight in space was on 28 April 2001.

TIPPING

Unit 9 *page 82* exercise **2**

The world's biggest tip
This story happened in an Italian restaurant in Madison Avenue in New York, when two businessmen from Wall Street celebrated a big business deal.

BUSINESS CARDS

Unit 9 *page 83* exercise **4**

A bad introduction
This story happened in October 2000 when Yasuo Tanaka started work as governor of Nagano in Japan. The other man in the story was very unhappy that he was his new boss.

WHAT DO YOU THINK?

Unit 10 *page 89* exercise **7**

Toy ducks – The main story is about new products.
Tony Blair's face with Margaret Thatcher's hair – The main story is about politics.
Unhappy face – The main story is about the Internet.
Ice melting in the Arctic – The main story is about the weather.

ADVERBS

1 Adverbs of frequency

never	rarely	sometimes	often	always
0%				100%

2 Other adverbs

We usually form adverbs by adding *-ly* to an adjective:
slow → *slow**ly***

There are some exceptions:
good → **well**

ARTICLES

1 *a* or *an*?

an + a e i o u
a + b c d f g h j k l m n p q r s t v w x y z

2 *a* or *the*?

When we talk about something for the first time, we usually use *a* or *an*:
*Can I have **an** apple, please?*

When we talk about it again, we usually use *the*:
*I'd like **the** small apple, please.*

3 Zero article

We don't use an article before most countries, languages and place names:
Portugal, English, Shanghai

CAN AND CAN'T

When something is possible or allowed, we use *can* + verb:
They can come.

When something is not possible or not allowed, we use *can't* + verb:
They can't come.

To ask if something is possible or allowed, we use the question form:
Can they come?

Note: *Can* is the same for all persons: *I/You/He/She/It/We/They can*

COMPARATIVE AND SUPERLATIVE ADJECTIVES

One-syllable adjectives:

ADJECTIVE	COMPARATIVE	SUPERLATIVE
cheap	cheap**er**	cheap**est**

Adjectives ending in *-y*:

ADJECTIVE	COMPARATIVE	SUPERLATIVE
easy	eas**ier**	eas**iest**

Adjectives with two or more syllables:

ADJECTIVE	COMPARATIVE	SUPERLATIVE
expensive	**more** expensive	**most** expensive

Irregular adjectives:

ADJECTIVE	COMPARATIVE	SUPERLATIVE
good	**better**	**best**
bad	**worse**	**worst**

Use *than* after comparatives:
*A is cheaper **than** B.*

Use *the* before superlatives:
*It's **the** smallest in the world.*

FUTURE (*going to*)

To talk about the future, use the present tense of *to be* + *going to* + verb.

➕	➖	❓
I'm going to have	I'm not going to have	Am I going to have?
You're going to have	You aren't going to have	Are you going to have?
He/She/It's going to have	He/She/It isn't going to have	Is he/she/it going to have?
We/They're going to have	We/They aren't going to have	Are we/they going to have?

HAVE TO AND DON'T HAVE TO

When something is necessary, we use *have to* + verb:
He has to go.

When something is not necessary, we use *don't / doesn't have to* + verb:
He doesn't have to go.

To ask if something is necessary, we use the question form:
Does he have to go?

NOUNS

1 Most nouns are countable and have singular and plural forms.

| one job | two jobs | one company | two compan**ies** |
| one person | two **people** | one man | two **men** |

2 Some nouns are uncountable and don't have a plural form.

information   money   space   water   electricity

We don't use *a* or *an* with uncountable nouns and they always take a singular verb.

3 *How many … ?* is used with countable nouns:
How many newspapers?
How much … ? is used with uncountable nouns:
How much information?

PAST SIMPLE

We use the past simple to talk about past, finished actions.

1 Positive form

For regular verbs add *-d* or *-ed*:
She realised.   You worked.

Some verbs are irregular in the positive form – see the list on page 120.

2 Negative and question forms

For negatives in the past, use *didn't* + verb:
*She **didn't** realise.   You **didn't** work.*

For questions use *did* + verb:
***Did** she realise?   **Did** you work?*

The past simple is the same for all persons, except *to be* (see page 105).

PRESENT CONTINUOUS

We use the present continuous to talk about things which are happening now. To form the present continuous, use the present tense of *to be* + verb *-ing*.

⊕	⊖	❓
I'm starting	I'm not starting	Am I starting?
You're starting	You're not starting	Are you starting?
He/She/It's starting	He/She/It isn't starting	Is he/she/it starting?
We/They're starting	We/They aren't starting	Are we/they starting?

PRESENT SIMPLE

We use the present simple to talk about things which are always or usually true.

⊕	⊖	❓
I work	I don't work	Do I work?
You work	You don't work	Do you work?
He/She/It works	He/She/It doesn't work	Does he/she/it work?
We/They work	We/They don't work	Do we/they work?

TO BE

1 Present

⊕	⊖	❓
I am	I'm not	Am I … ?
You are	You aren't	Are you … ?
He/She/It is	He/She/It isn't	Is he/she/it … ?
We/They are	We/They aren't	Are we/they … ?

Note: In the negative form *You're not*, *He's not*, etc. is also possible.

2 Past

⊕	⊖	❓
I was	I wasn't	Was I … ?
You were	You weren't	Were you … ?
He/She/It was	He/She/It wasn't	Was he/she/it … ?
We/They were	We/They weren't	Were we/they … ?

transcripts

1 introductions

page 4   exercise 3   (CD Track 1)

PATRICIA   Good morning. It's 10 o'clock and this is the news. I'm Patricia da Gama. There are problems for President George W Bush …

WOMAN   Hello.
MAN   Good afternoon. It's Paul de Gromoboy here. I'm from International Media.
WOMAN   I'm sorry …
MAN   It's Paul de Gromoboy …
WOMAN   No, no, I'm sorry, are you a salesperson?
MAN   Er … um …
WOMAN   Are you a salesperson?
MAN   Well, yes, yes, I am.
WOMAN   Thank you, but I'm not interested. Goodbye.

DAVID   Hello. I'm David. Pleased to meet you.
JULIA   Oh, hi. I'm Julia.
DAVID   Yes … so … er … how are you?
JULIA   Fine, thank you … Fine … Bye.
DAVID   Oh … Goodbye.

ANSWERPHONE
Hello. This is Ravi Shipman. I'm not here at the moment, but please leave your name and number. Thank you.

PILOT   Good evening. This is your captain speaking. My name's Roger Harper. Welcome aboard flight 27409 to Grand Cayman … I'm sorry. Welcome aboard … Welcome … ooh … er … just a moment, please.

page 8   exercise 1   (CD Track 2)

CARLOS   Pedro, I'd like you to meet Tanya.
PEDRO   How do you do?
CARLOS   Tanya, this is Pedro.
TANYA   Pleased to meet you.
PEDRO   So, Tanya, which company are you with?
TANYA   I'm with Telecom International. Who do you work for?
PEDRO   The same company. Telecom International!

page 8   exercise 3   (CD Track 3)

ENRICO   Teresa! Good to see you again. How are you?
TERESA   Fine, thank you. How are you?
ENRICO   Very well, thank you. So, how's business?
TERESA   Oh, OK. I'm very busy at the moment.
ENRICO   Good to hear it. Anyway, see you soon!
TERESA   Yes, see you!

page 9   exercise 5   (CD Track 4)

RECEPTIONIST   Hello, Telecom International.
RAYMOND   Oh, hello. Can I speak to Dorota Celaeno, please?
RECEPTIONIST   Of course. What's your name, please?
RAYMOND   It's Raymond Merope, from Atlas Products.
RECEPTIONIST   Just a moment, please. … I'm sorry, she's not in the office today.
RAYMOND   Oh, OK. No problem. Goodbye.

page 10/11   exercise **1/2**   (CD Track 5)

NEWS PRESENTER

Good morning. It's ten o'clock and this is the news. I'm Patricia da Gama.

There are problems for President George W Bush at the start of his three-day visit to Japan.

100,000 people are in Denmark today for the Roskilde rock festival.

And Angelina Jolie is in London tonight for her new film *Gone in 60 seconds*.

Business news. It's a good day on the stock market. In New York, the stock market is up forty-seven points.

But the euro is down eight cents against the dollar.

And sport. It's bad news for Manchester United. They are out of the European Cup, after losing 4 – 2 at home to Galataseray.

page 11   PRONUNCIATION   (CD Track 6)

A   six   three   ten   eight
     fifty   thirteen   twenty   eighteen

B   meeting   see   please
     name   plane   today
     film   business   captain
     well   festival   hello

2 people

page 12   PRONUNCIATION   (CD Track 7)

boss   business   city   customer
employees   factories   office   managers
person   shops

page 13   exercise **4**   (CD Track 8)

Hanae Mori is from Japan and her homes are in Paris and Tokyo. She's in the fashion business and she's the boss of Hanae Mori International. It's an international company with hundreds of employees. Her clothes are for women and her customers are from many different countries. She has shops in many of the world's big cities, including New York, Paris and Tokyo.

page 17   exercise **3**   (CD Track 9)

A   B   C   D   E   F   G   H   I   J
K   L   M   N   O   P   Q   R   S
T   U   V   W   X   Y   Z

page 17   PRONUNCIATION   (CD Track 10)

A   job   phone   number
     dot   slowly   company

B   hotel   home   clothes   from
     customer   country   what   shop
     boss   son   husband   mother
     Tokyo   London   brother   clock

page 19   exercise **3/4**   (CD Track 11)

ASSISTANT   Yes. Can I help you?
CUSTOMER   Hello. I'd like a chicken sandwich, please.
ASSISTANT   Just chicken?
CUSTOMER   Er ... well, what's this?
ASSISTANT   That's avocado. It's very good with chicken.
CUSTOMER   Hmm. Avocado. And what are those?
ASSISTANT   Those are prawns.

CUSTOMER   OK. Can I have a chicken and prawn sandwich?

ASSISTANT   How about some tomatoes with that?

CUSTOMER   Tomatoes? Hmm. OK. Why not?

ASSISTANT   Right. One chicken, prawn and tomato sandwich!

CUSTOMER   And I'd like an orange as well, please.

ASSISTANT   Sorry. Can you say that again, please?

CUSTOMER   I'd like an orange juice as well.

ASSISTANT   One orange juice!

CUSTOMER   How much is it?

ASSISTANT   It's $5.50. Thank you very much.

review 1

page 21   **PRONUNCIATION**   (CD Track 12)

A business   person
       best   place

B A plate of prawns, please.
       My boss's brother's bar.
       Help, please! It's a big problem.

C her   your
       who   USA

D Who's your new employee?
       Do you have a home in the USA?
       Yes, we have your number here.

3 jobs

page 22   exercise **5**   (CD Track 13)

Conversation 1

DEBORAH   So what about the money? $40,000 a year. Is that right?

TREVOR   Well, I earn $40,000 a year. But I work very, very hard and I sell a lot of advertising.

DEBORAH   So?

TREVOR   So I earn my money because I'm good at my job.

DEBORAH   I see.

TREVOR   In this job, you earn money when you sell.

DEBORAH   And when you don't sell …

TREVOR   … you don't earn any money.

DEBORAH   Oh, I see. Oh, well, thank you, Trevor. Goodbye.

TREVOR   Goodbye.

Conversation 2

CAROLE   Hmm. So you know the oil industry, Mr Heywood, but what languages do you speak?

MR HEYWOOD   Oh, well, I speak English.

CAROLE   English.

MR HEYWOOD   Yes. I speak English very well.

CAROLE   And what about Spanish?

MR HEYWOOD   Spanish? Er … no.

CAROLE   Spanish is very important in this job, Mr Heywood.

MR HEYWOOD   Yes. I see. Well, no problem. Lessons.

CAROLE   Lessons.

MR HEYWOOD   Yes, Spanish lessons. Easy.

CAROLE   I'm sorry, Mr Heywood, you're not the person for us.

MR HEYWOOD   Oh, well, thank you, Carole. Goodbye.

CAROLE   Goodbye, Mr Heywood.

page 26   **PRONUNCIATION**   (CD Track 14)

a meeting on Monday morning
never in the afternoon

page 27   exercise **3**   (CD Track 15)

ANSWERPHONE
Hello. This is Philippe Sebald at Lost River.com. I'm not here at the moment, but please leave your name and number. Thank you.

MESSAGE 1

Philippe, hello. It's Dima here, from the accounts department. It's about your expenses for the New York trip. Can we have a meeting on Monday afternoon? Is two forty-five OK with you? Goodbye.

MESSAGE 2

Hi, Philippe, this is Imran here. How about lunch some time next week? Maybe Wednesday at half past one? Call me in the office on 48769. Thanks. See you!

MESSAGE 3

Oh, hello, Mr Sebald. My name's Birgit van der Gouwe. I'm a salesperson with Lightweight Industries. Thank you for your call. I can meet you next week. … Tuesday is OK with me. Is three o'clock in the afternoon possible? Thank you very much. Goodbye!

MESSAGE 4

Hi, Philippe, it's Bruno here. I'm in town this weekend. How about a meeting on Sunday? Two forty-five? Three o'clock? I know, I know, it's Sunday, but … well, hope it's OK with you. Call me at the New York office. Bye now.

page 27   exercise **5/6**   (CD Track 16)

BRUNO	Hi. Bruno Ponzi.
PHILIPPE	Hello, Bruno. It's Philippe here.
BRUNO	Hey, Philippe. How are you?
PHILIPPE	Fine, thanks, fine. Bruno, it's about this meeting on Sunday. I'm sorry but I can't meet you then. I never work on Sunday. How about Saturday? Can we meet on Saturday afternoon?
BRUNO	Saturday afternoon's OK. Two o'clock?
PHILIPPE	Can you make it two fifteen?
BRUNO	Two fifteen's great. At the office?
PHILIPPE	Sure. See you there.
BRUNO	Great. See you.

page 28   exercise **1/2**   (CD Track 17)

SECRETARY	Good afternoon, sales and marketing.
LISA	Oh, hello. I'd like to speak to Alan, please.
SECRETARY	Yes, of course. Can I have your name, please?
LISA	Yes. It's Lisa.
SECRETARY	I'm sorry. Can you say that again, please?
LISA	Yes. It's Lisa. Lisa Castle. You know, Alan's boss. And I'd like to speak to him, please.
SECRETARY	Yes. Yes, of course. I'm sorry, Lisa. Just a moment, please.

page 28   exercise **3**   (CD Track 18)

ALAN	Yes!
SECRETARY	Alan. I'm sorry to interrupt, but there's a phone call for you.
ALAN	Oh! Who is it?
SECRETARY	I'm afraid it's the boss.
ALAN	Oh, no. Can you tell her I'm in a meeting?
SECRETARY	What? Again?
ALAN	Well … tell her I'm at lunch.
SECRETARY	Is that a good excuse?
ALAN	No. … Well, you think of something then.
SECRETARY	Thank you very much.

page 29   exercise **5/6**   (CD Track 19)

SECRETARY	Hello? I'm afraid that Alan's with a customer at the moment. Would you like to leave a message?
LISA	Yes. Can you tell him it's Lisa? And can you ask him to call me? My number's 777 9876.
SECRETARY	Certainly.
LISA	Thank you.
SECRETARY	You're welcome. Goodbye.

4 places

page 31   exercise **2**   (CD Track 20)

STUDENT   The Loyola Law School? I love it. I think it's a really interesting building. I mean, it's new and it's beautiful. The street? It's nothing special. It's a quiet street, it's usually clean. You know, it's a good area. It's not a rich area, but it's safe. And the car? Actually, that's my car. I always park there on Tuesdays. OK, it's not an expensive car, but it's very, very fast. So, today's weather? Well, it's cold and it's dull. It's a good day to study, I guess.

page 31   **PRONUNCIATION**   (CD Track 21)

A school   car   short
   beautiful   are   boring

B Are you a student?   Park your car here.
   Do you like it?   New York Law School.

page 34   exercise **3**   (CD Track 22)

ERICA   Hi, Mois! Welcome to Brazil! I'm sorry, but we can't meet at the country club at 12:30. Can we meet at the office instead? At about 1:15? How do you get there? OK. Go out of your hotel and turn left, walk along the beach and then turn left into Vinicius de Morais … it's the third turning, I think. OK. Then, go past the Girl from Ipanema bar and the office is on the next corner. It has a big sign outside, so you can't miss it. See you there! … Oh, my mobile number is 06878 098778. Bye!

page 37   exercise **3**   (CD Track 23)

WOMAN 1   When you go into the Chelsea Hotel in New York, you know you're in a special place. Its guests include many of the world's most famous names: Bob Dylan, Jimi Hendrix, Andy Warhol … The Chelsea's right in the centre of the city, so there are very good transport links. And, of course, the world's best shops, theatres and nightclubs are all around you. There are more than four hundred rooms and suites in the hotel, but you can only stay in about a hundred of them. That's because a lot of people like the Chelsea so much that they actually live there!

MAN   The Oriental, Bangkok in Thailand has more than a hundred years' experience in the hotel business. That means it knows what businesspeople want. It has conference rooms for big meetings and meeting rooms for small ones. For private meetings there are also a lot of suites – the biggest is more than three hundred square metres!

WOMAN 2   Sweden's Ice Hotel is a very different kind of hotel. They make it from snow and ice every December and it stays open until May. That's when the weather gets hotter and the hotel simply melts and disappears. The hotel has an Ice Sauna, an Ice Cinema and if you want a drink in the Ice Bar, it even comes in an ice glass. There's just one problem with the Ice Hotel: it's very cold! The temperature in the suites and bedrooms is between minus four and minus nine degrees Celsius.

page 37   **PRONUNCIATION**   (CD Track 24)

room rates   health club   hotel restaurant
Chelsea Hotel   luxury location
transport links   conference rooms

review 2

page 39 exercise **4** (CD Track 25)

INSTRUCTOR

All right, are you ready? … Right, out of the door. Now! Come on, out of that door! Go round the post. Round it! Now through the tunnel! Through! Through! Through! Come on, come on! Up the steps! Up! And across the bridge! Come on, across the bridge! Now, down the slope! Down the slope! And along the path now! Come on! Along the path! Right! Into the building! Into the building, now!

page 39 **PRONUNCIATION** (CD Track 26)

A get   call
   guide   quiet
B good   cold   bank

5 speed and power

page 41 exercise **4** (CD Track 27)

REPORTER

For tourists and businesspeople, Dubai is one of the most popular places in the Middle East. There are some fantastic facilities for businesspeople and, for tourists, there are a lot of great hotels, beaches and shops.

Transport in Dubai is not a problem. There's a big new airport, there are a lot of taxis and there are also some buses. But I'm afraid there aren't any trains and, of course, there aren't any bicycles, because it's very, very hot!

But in this city, there's really only one way to travel – the car. People in Dubai love their cars. And there's a good reason for this: petrol here is very cheap. So, there are always a lot of cars on the streets and there are some very noisy motorbikes, too!

And for people who want the old Dubai, there are still some camels here!

page 43 **PRONUNCIATION** (CD Track 28)

A star   Tokyo   shop
   space   Internet   information
B Russia   sea   accommodation
   Singapore   bottle   water   electricity
   English   lot

page 47 exercise **4** (CD Track 29)

RESEARCHER Hello. I'm doing a survey of work and leisure time. Can I ask you some questions?

MAN Yeah, all right.

RESEARCHER How many hours a week do you normally work?

MAN I work about … oh, about fifty hours a week.

RESEARCHER So, how much free time do you have?

MAN Oooh. About … can I think about this for a moment? … Yeah, about thirty hours.

RESEARCHER Thirty hours. And how do you spend your free time?

MAN Well, I spend about two hours a day watching TV, so what's that?

RESEARCHER About fourteen hours a week?

MAN Yeah.

RESEARCHER And how do you spend the rest of your free time?

MAN I don't know … I probably spend about an hour a day talking to family or friends … no, more than that. You know, on the phone or socialising or whatever.

RESEARCHER So, about ten hours?

MAN Yeah. That sounds about right. Then I spend about, maybe, three hours a week reading … and the rest of the time? I probably spend the rest of the time doing nothing at all. Do you know what I mean?

RESEARCHER Yes, yes, I do.

page 47 PRONUNCIATION (CD Track 30)

slowing down   watching television
having fun   working in the garden

6 business and pleasure

page 48   exercise **2/5**   (CD Track 31)

PRESENTER   And before we finish today's programme, let's take our normal trip around the world. Today, we start in the USA, with New York City. Hello, New York, what's happening with you?

USA   Yes, good morning! It's early here in New York – it's just 7 am. The sun's coming up and we're getting ready for the day.

PRESENTER   And what about down in South America, in Brazil? Are you ready for the day, as well?

BRAZIL   Yes, we certainly are. It's the end of the morning rush hour here in São Paulo. It's nine o'clock right now and everyone's starting work.

PRESENTER   And on the other side of the Atlantic Ocean, what about Morocco? Good morning, Casablanca, what's the weather like with you?

MOROCCO   Hello. Good morning. The temperature is rising in Casablanca, it's eleven o'clock and I can tell you it's pretty hot here already.

PRESENTER   Now, let's go north, to France. Hello, Paris. How are you?

FRANCE   We're fine, thank you. Here in Paris, it's one o'clock and, in fact, we're having lunch. Cheers!

PRESENTER   Cheers! And, what's happening further east, in Russia? Can you hear us in Moscow?

RUSSIA   Yes, we can hear you very well. Here in Moscow it's three in the afternoon and I'm afraid that already it's getting dark and it's getting cold.

PRESENTER   Next, we go to Pakistan. Hello, Karachi!

PAKISTAN   Good afternoon to you. Well, in Karachi, it's the end of the working day. It's 5 pm, the stock market is closing and people are leaving their offices.

PRESENTER   And I guess it's the end of the working day in China as well. What's happening in Beijing at the moment?

CHINA   Yes, it's eight o'clock in the evening here in Beijing. The sun is setting and everyone's relaxing at the end of the day.

PRESENTER   And finally, to Japan. Are you ready for bed in Tokyo?

JAPAN   No, we aren't. It's 9 pm in Tokyo but we're still working!

PRESENTER   Thank you, Tokyo. Well, wherever you are in the world – good morning, good afternoon, good evening, and from me, goodbye!

page 50/51   exercise **2/3**   (CD Track 32)

The woman in the photograph is Christine Edwards. So, what's she doing? Well, she isn't advertising a new product, she isn't making a programme for children's TV and she isn't appearing in a show at the theatre. In fact, she's wearing a giraffe costume because she's running in the London marathon. At the same time, she's also raising a lot of money for charity.

Christine comes from Wales in the west of the UK and she works as an administrator. But every year she runs the London marathon in a funny costume. Although she's smiling at the camera and she's waving her arms, she's feeling very tired at the moment. Her costume is over three metres tall and it's very hot inside. But the worst thing is that the marathon usually takes her more than seven hours!

page 52 exercise **1/3** (CD Track 33)

CUSTOMER   Good morning.

ASSISTANT   Yeah. What do you want?

CUSTOMER   I'm looking for a wetsuit.

ASSISTANT   Well, you're in the wrong shop.

CUSTOMER   But it says in the window that you sell wetsuits.

ASSISTANT   Yeah. Well that's because the manager's an idiot.

CUSTOMER   Oh … I see. Well, do you sell surfboards?

ASSISTANT   No, of course not.

CUSTOMER   What? Are you joking? This shop is Surfer's Paradise, right? And you're telling me that you don't sell surfboards.

ASSISTANT   Yeah.

CUSTOMER   I see. Well, where can I buy a surfboard?

ASSISTANT   I've no idea.

CUSTOMER   Right. Well, thank you very much. Goodbye.

ASSISTANT   Yeah. And don't come back.

page 53 exercise **4** (CD Track 34)

CUSTOMER   Good morning.

ASSISTANT   Hello. Can I help you?

CUSTOMER   I'm looking for a wetsuit.

ASSISTANT   I'm sorry, but we don't sell wetsuits.

CUSTOMER   But it says in the window that you sell wetsuits.

ASSISTANT   Yes. I'm afraid that sign's a mistake.

CUSTOMER   Oh … I see. Well, do you sell surfboards?

ASSISTANT   No, I'm afraid we don't.

CUSTOMER   What? Are you joking? This shop is Surfer's Paradise, right? And you're telling me that you don't sell surfboards.

ASSISTANT   Yes, I know it's crazy, but we're having problems with our supplier.

CUSTOMER   I see. Well, where can I buy a surfboard?

ASSISTANT   Why don't you try the shop across the road?

CUSTOMER   Right. Well, thank you very much. Goodbye.

ASSISTANT   Goodbye. Have a nice day.

page 53 exercise **6** (CD Track 35)

ASSISTANT   Hi! Can I help you?

CUSTOMER   Hello. I'm looking for a wetsuit. Do you sell them?

ASSISTANT   Of course we do. Hey, this is a surf shop!

CUSTOMER   Great!

ASSISTANT   How about these?

CUSTOMER   Oh, yeah! I like this one … and this one. Can I try them on?

ASSISTANT   Sure. The changing room's just through there. … So, what do you think?

CUSTOMER   Great! Can I have this one, please?

ASSISTANT   Sure. That one's $150. Is that OK?

CUSTOMER   Yeah. Can I pay by credit card?

ASSISTANT   No problem.

CUSTOMER   Oh … and can I have a receipt?

ASSISTANT   Sure … Just sign there.

page 53 PRONUNCIATION (CD Track 36)

A cash   nice   the   good
   and   try   afraid   look

B across   racquet   bad   right   buy
   sign   manager   supplier polite
   woman   put

review 3

page 57 **PRONUNCIATION** (CD Track 37)

A shop   cheap
conversation   check
machine   watch

B children's show   charity shop
how much cash?   fish for lunch

C pleasure   joke
usually   Germany

D giraffe   television   decision   job

7 technology

page 59 exercise **4** (CD Track 38)

The first e-mail
The American computer scientist, Ray Tomlinson, was the first person to send an e-mail. It was some time in 1971, but he can't remember exactly when. It wasn't big news at the time because the two computers were in the same room. And his message wasn't very interesting – it was just: 'QWERTYUIOP'. Why? Was this a new computer language? No, they were the letters at the top of his computer's keyboard!

page 60 exercise **2** (CD Track 39)

The first phone call
The first phone call was on March 10 1875, when Alexander Graham Bell, the inventor of the telephone, called his assistant. His first words were, 'Mr Watson, come here, I want you.'

Bell and Watson realised that their phone was a fantastic business idea. They showed it to some American businessmen and asked for $100,000. But the businessmen laughed: 'It's just an electrical toy.'

So Bell started his own company and soon, with the name American Telephone and Telegraph, it was the top company in the USA.

page 61 exercise **4** (CD Track 40)

The first tourist in space
For many years Dennis Tito was a top American businessman. During his career, he made millions and millions of dollars. But he always had a dream – to be an astronaut. So, one day, he asked the American space agency NASA, 'How much does it cost to go into space?' The answer was: 'Sorry. Space is not for tourists.'

So, Tito went to the Russians and asked them the same question. The Russians weren't sure. 'How about $20 million?' asked Tito. This time, the answer was 'Yes'.

And so in April 2001, Tito left from Baikonur, Kazakhstan in a Russian Soyuz-TM rocket and flew to the International Space Station. While he was in space, Tito had a fantastic time, just like a normal tourist!

page 63 exercise **4/5** (CD Track 41)

RUUDI	Hello, IT helpline. I'm Ruudi. How can I help you?
TAMARA	Oh, hello. Yes. There's a problem with my computer.
RUUDI	Can I take your name and phone number, please?
TAMARA	Yes. I'm Tamara Vela and my number's 555 7785.
RUUDI	Thank you. Which system do you have?
TAMARA	Er … it's a laptop.
RUUDI	No, I'm sorry, which system do you have? You know, is it Apple, Windows, Linux?
TAMARA	Oh, I'm sorry. It's Windows 2000.
RUUDI	Right. So, what's the problem?
TAMARA	Well, last night the screen suddenly went blank and all my work just disappeared.
RUUDI	OK. Are you sitting in front of the computer now?
TAMARA	Yes, I am.
RUUDI	And is the computer on?
TAMARA	Yes, of course.
RUUDI	OK. What's on the screen at the moment?

TAMARA	There's nothing there.
RUUDI	And what happens when you move the mouse?
TAMARA	Er … nothing.
RUUDI	OK, on the keyboard can you press Alt and Delete?
TAMARA	At the same time?
RUUDI	Yes.
TAMARA	Er … nothing, it's still blank.
RUUDI	Just a moment, Tamara … actually, can I call you back?
TAMARA	Oh. OK, sure.
RUUDI	Two minutes, OK? Bye.
TAMARA	Bye.

8 careers

page 66   exercise **3**   (CD Track 42)

TAMMY VO

At school I was very interested in math and physics. They were my favourite subjects. So, when I went to university, I studied electrical engineering. At the end of the course I stayed at university for another year and did some research into systems management.

Anyway, then I left university in 2001 and worked as the night manager of a 24-hour store. It wasn't a fantastic job, but I made some money and after a while I heard about a great opportunity: a computer company in California wanted a young electrical engineer for a new project. So I sent a resume and a letter. Two weeks later I had an interview and the next day they offered me the job. So I joined the company and moved to California. Yeah, it's a good life here, but now I feel I want a change …

page 66   exercise **4**   (CD Track 43)

At school I was very interested in math and physics. They were my favourite subjects. So, when I went to university, I studied electrical engineering. At the end of the course I stayed at university for

another year and did some research into systems management.

page 67   exercise **5**   (CD Track 44)

Anyway, then I left university in 2001 and worked as the night manager of a 24-hour store. It wasn't a fantastic job, but I made some money and after a while I heard about a great opportunity: a computer company in California wanted a young electrical engineer for a new project. So I sent a resume and a letter. Two weeks later I had an interview and the next day they offered me the job. So I joined the company and moved to California. Yeah, it's a good life here, but now I feel I want a change …

page 68/69   exercise **4/5**   (CD Track 45)

WOMAN	So, tell me about yourself. Where were you born?
MAN	I was born in Addis Ababa.
WOMAN	Ethiopia?
MAN	Right.
WOMAN	And where did you grow up?
MAN	I grew up in New York. My father worked for the United Nations.
WOMAN	Really? So did you grow up in Manhattan?
MAN	No. No, I didn't. I grew up in Queens. That was where we lived.
WOMAN	Interesting. So, where did you go to school?
MAN	I went to school at Haddonfield High.
WOMAN	OK. So, tell me about your work experience. What was your first job?
MAN	Well, I went to university at Harvard and then I got a job as a consultant with McKinsey in Philadelphia.
WOMAN	McKinsey? Wow! That's a good company … and now you're with a small company in … where? … Vancouver? Is that right?
MAN	Yes. Yes, it is.
WOMAN	So, when did you join your present company?
MAN	I joined them in … er … February 2002.

WOMAN   And why did you leave your last job?

MAN   Well, it was tough at McKinsey. I have a young family and I didn't like the long hours.

WOMAN   And tell me about your present job …

page 69   **PRONUNCIATION**   (CD Track 46)

A   work   where   how   appear
were   there   about   experience

B   first   research   here   thirty
dear   wear   airport   idea
thousand   house   now   word

page 70   exercise **1**   (CD Track 47)

BOSS   OK, Martha, what can you show me?

MARTHA   Well, this graph shows our sales figures for the year. As you can see, January was a good month. Sales went up. Sales stayed the same in February and March, and then in April they went down.

page 70/71   exercise **3/4**   (CD Track 48)

BOSS   Excuse me, Martha, did you say 'they went down in April'? Why did they go down?

MARTHA   Well, there are two reasons, really. Er … we had a problem with a big customer.

BOSS   Which one?

MARTHA   Wiley's in London.

BOSS   OK. What was it?

MARTHA   He didn't pay us for his last order, so we didn't …

BOSS   What? Why didn't he pay us?

MARTHA   I don't know. I'm sorry. I asked him but he didn't really explain. He just called me one day and said he didn't have the money.

BOSS   He didn't have the money?

MARTHA   I'm sorry, I …

BOSS   OK. OK. What's the other reason?

MARTHA   Um … there weren't any new products in the shops.

BOSS   I don't believe this. Why weren't there any new products in the shops?

MARTHA   Well, there was a problem at the factory in March so we didn't have the products in the warehouse.

BOSS   What? That's crazy! Why didn't you do something?

MARTHA   I wasn't here at the time so I didn't know about it.

BOSS   Why weren't you here?

MARTHA   I was on holiday.

BOSS   Oh, I see. Well, why didn't you tell me about this when you got back?

MARTHA   I didn't tell you because you were in America.

BOSS   So, why didn't you phone me?

MARTHA   I tried to call you, but you were always in a meeting.

BOSS   Why didn't you send an e-mail? Why didn't you leave a message?

MARTHA   I … I didn't leave a message because … because I didn't want you to know.

BOSS   Well, I know now and I'm not happy.

MARTHA   Yes. I … I don't know what to say.

page 72   exercise **4**   (CD Track 49)

In 1986, Kao heard about some interesting research at the Harvard Medical School. A professor showed him how he grew sheets of human skin in his laboratory. Because Kao was a doctor and also knew about business, he saw an opportunity. He took the professor's idea and started a small bio-tech company.

'I did everything,' said Kao. 'I wrote the business plan, I got the money and I employed the managers.'

Before long, Kao's small company was worth millions of dollars.

Over the next few years, Kao started more small companies. He also wrote a successful book about his ideas, called *Jamming*. When other businesspeople read his book, they came to him and asked for his advice. By 1996 Kao was so busy that he stopped teaching at the Harvard Business School and started a company called Idea Factory.

Today, Idea Factory is a way for Kao to share his ideas and his advice with other businesspeople. It's also a way for him to make a very good profit!

review 4

page 75 PRONUNCIATION (CD Track 50)

A do   two
    day   today
    doctor   teacher

B showed   asked   started

C watched   appeared   interrupted
    realised   laughed   finished   played
    visited   listened

9 on the **move**

page 76 PRONUNCIATION (CD Track 51)

A flight   visa   where
    traffic   driving   network

B foreign office   platform fifty-five
    travel advisor   working women
    the world's worst visitor

page 77 exercise **3** (CD Track 52)

PASSENGER Good morning. Can I check in for Kuala Lumpur, please?

CLERK Of course. Can I see your ticket and your passport, please? … Thank you. Are you checking in any luggage?

PASSENGER Yes. These two suitcases.

CLERK OK. And do you have any hand luggage?

PASSENGER Just this.

CLERK Good. Now, I'm afraid there's a short delay on the flight this morning. So, can you go to boarding gate 32 at 11:55? Here's your boarding pass.

PASSENGER Thank you.

CLERK Have a good flight.

page 77 exercise **4** (CD Track 53)

MAN Good morning, everybody. I'm sorry I'm late.

WOMAN What was the problem this time?

MAN I'm sorry. The police stopped me and I didn't have my driving licence.

WOMAN What? I don't believe this. Yesterday you were late because there was an accident, the day before you were in a traffic jam.

MAN I'm sorry. I'm having a bad week.

WOMAN Yes, you are. How about coming to work by bus tomorrow?

page 78 exercise **2** (CD Track 54)

ASSISTANT Yes, mate, how can I help you?

TOURIST Yes, hello. We're trying to get to Darwin. We have to be there before tomorrow evening. Er … can we take a train?

ASSISTANT Sorry, mate. There aren't any trains in Katherine.

TOURIST Oh, I see.

ASSISTANT What about a bus?

TOURIST Oh, no. I don't think so. We don't like buses.

ASSISTANT Well, you have to hire a car, then, mate.

TOURIST Can we hire one today?

ASSISTANT Yes, you can. But you have to have an international driving licence.

TOURIST That's OK. I have one of those.

ASSISTANT And do you carry a gun?

TOURIST No … no … I …

ASSISTANT You have to be careful of the crocodiles, you know.

TOURIST Really? Are you serious?

ASSISTANT Am I serious? … Of course not! I'm only joking, mate. They ate three tourists last week, so they're not that hungry any more.

page 79 exercise **3** (CD Track 55)

REPORTER

Singapore has one of the best international airports in the world and, for most people, it's very easy to get into and out of the country. Visitors don't usually have to get a visa and you certainly don't have to worry about health problems while you're here.

When you're out of the airport, transport in Singapore is no problem. It's a small place and there's an excellent public transport system. My advice is – use it. But if you have to hire a car, remember that you have to pay to use some roads and you have to buy a special licence to drive in the downtown area. Oh … and you also have to drive on the left. It's important to remember that!

And just two final points. Singapore is a very clean city and the government wants to keep it that way. So, if you're a smoker, you have to be careful. You can't smoke in public places – even when you're waiting for a bus. And if you like chewing gum, forget it. You can't even bring chewing gum into the country.

page 82 exercise **2** (CD Track 56)

The world's biggest tip

In this city, you always have to leave a tip. When you take a cab, you usually give the driver a 10 per cent tip. When you have a haircut, you leave the hairdresser 15 per cent. And when you eat in a restaurant, the waiter usually gets a 20 per cent tip. Usually – but not always.

In April 2001, two businessmen walked into one of the city's busiest restaurants after a very good day's work. They said to the waiter, 'We'd like to buy a drink for everyone here.' Then they ordered a very, very expensive meal. When they asked for the check, the waiter was worried: it was for around $9,000.

But the check wasn't a problem for the two businessmen. They were happy to pay and they even added a tip of $15,000 for the waiter!

page 83 exercise **4** (CD Track 57)

A bad introduction

It was the boss's first day in his new job, so he walked around the office and introduced himself to everyone. He offered his business card to each person in the usual way: he held it with two hands, so that the other person could read it easily.

But one man in the office said, 'I don't want your business card. I already know who you are.'

'Please take it,' said the boss and smiled.

Slowly, the man took the business card … and then he folded it in two.

Everyone in the office knew that this was very rude. When you receive a business card in this country, you always have to read it very carefully.

In fact, the next day the story was in the newspapers and the boss got more than 10,000 e-mails of support from people right across the country.

10 in the **news**

page 86 exercise **1/2** (CD Track 58)

DJ

Now the weather. Well, it's going to be a lovely day in San Berdino today. We're going to see a lot of sunshine, and if you're out this afternoon, you're going to feel the heat! Forty-two degrees is today's top temperature!

Travel news. After yesterday's problems at San Berdino Airport, the situation is returning to normal this morning. There aren't going to be any more cancellations, although I'm afraid there are going to be some delays on international flights.

On the roads, no problems! But don't forget the big match at the City Stadium this evening. It's the S B Bluesocks against D C Thumpers, so there's going to be a lot of traffic around the stadium just before 7:00.

page 88   exercise **2/3/6**   (CD Track 59)

BRIAN   Hello there.

MIRA   Oh, hello, Brian.

ANGIE   Hi, Brian.

BRIAN   So what are you two talking about?

ANGIE   Well, the announcement, of course.

BRIAN   The announcement?

MIRA   Yes, there's going to be an announcement this afternoon.

ANGIE   And I think it's really important.

MIRA   That's right. That's what everyone's saying.

BRIAN   Oh, really. What's it about?

ANGIE   Well, we don't know. But I think it's going to be bad news. My guess is there are going to be some more job cuts.

MIRA   That's nonsense. I'm sure it's going to be good news. I reckon it's going to be a product launch or something like that.

ANGIE   What do you think, Brian?

BRIAN   Well, I'm sorry, but I don't agree with either of you. In my opinion, nothing's going to change. We have these announcements every six months. They're always the same.

MIRA   Oh, right. Well, thanks for that, Brian.

review 5

page 93   **PRONUNCIATION**   (CD Track 60)

A three   there
       bath   clothes

B thank you   than   another   nothing
       thirty   they   the   think

Phonemic symbols

Vowels

SYMBOL	EXAMPLES		PAGE
/ɑː/	car	park	31
/æ/	cash	and	53
/aɪ/	nice	try	53
/aʊ/	how	about	69
/e/	ten	twenty	11
/eɪ/	eight	day	11
/eə/	air	there	69
/ɪ/	six	fifty	11
/iː/	three	thirteen	11
/ɪə/	near	appear	69
/ɒ/	job	dot	17
/əʊ/	phone	slowly	17
/ɔː/	boring	short	31
/ʊ/	good	look	53
/uː/	school	beautiful	31
/ɜː/	work	were	69
/ʌ/	number	company	17
/ə/	the	afraid	53

Consonants

SYMBOL	EXAMPLES		PAGE
/b/	business	best	21
/d/	day	doctor	75
/f/	fifty	flight	76
/g/	get	good	39
/h/	her	who	21
/j/	your	yes	21
/k/	call	cold	39
/l/	link	location	37
/m/	meet	Monday	26
/n/	never	down	26, 47
/p/	person	place	21
/r/	room	restaurant	37
/s/	star	space	12, 43
/t/	time	want	43, 75
/v/	visa	visitor	76
/w/	work	women	76
/z/	zero	business	12
/ʃ/	shop	information	43, 57
/ʒ/	pleasure	usually	57
/ŋ/	having	working	47
/tʃ/	cheap	check	57
/θ/	three	bath	93
/ð/	there	clothes	93
/dʒ/	job	Germany	57

Irregular verbs

INFINITIVE	PAST TENSE		INFINITIVE	PAST TENSE		INFINITIVE	PAST TENSE
be	was/were		give	gave		rise	rose
buy	bought		go	went		say	said
come	came		grow	grew		see	saw
cost	cost		have	had		sell	sold
do	did		hear	heard		send	sent
drink	drank		know	knew		speak	spoke
drive	drove		learn	learnt		spend	spent
eat	ate		leave	left		take	took
fall	fell		lose	lost		teach	taught
find	found		make	made		tell	told
fly	flew		meet	met		think	thought
forget	forgot		pay	paid		win	won
get	got		read	read		write	wrote